Dollmaking

with Papier Mâché
and Paper Clay

DORIS ROCKWELL GOTTILLY

Krause Publications

700 East State St., Iola, WI 54990-0001
Telephone 715-445-2214
www.krause.com

Please call or write for our free catalog of publications. Our toll-free number to place an order or obtain a free catalog is 800-258-0929 or please use our regular business telephone 715-445-2214 for editorial comment and further information.

Designed by Jan Wojtech
Photography by Ross Hubbard (Krause Publications), Lynn Kennon, Jennifer Gottilly, Doris Rockwell Gottilly

Manufactured in the United States of America

Library of Congress Cataloging-in-Publication Data

Gottilly, Doris Rockwell
    Dollmaking with papier mâché and paper clay

    p. 160

    ISBN: 0-87341-586-8

    1. dollmaking   2. papier mâché   3. paper clay

                                                97-80615

DEDICATION

I would like to dedicate this book
in loving memory of my mother
Louise and with love to:
My sisters Lucia and Lucille.
My brothers Earl, Vinton,
Vernon, and Eugene.
My husband John.
My children Patricia, Kathleen,
John, Linda, Jennifer, and my
daughter-in-law Sheryl.
My grandchildren Gregory,
Zachary, Matthew, William,
Melinda, Cameron, and Jonathan
and all the rest of my family and
friends. All of their faces are
reflected in my work.

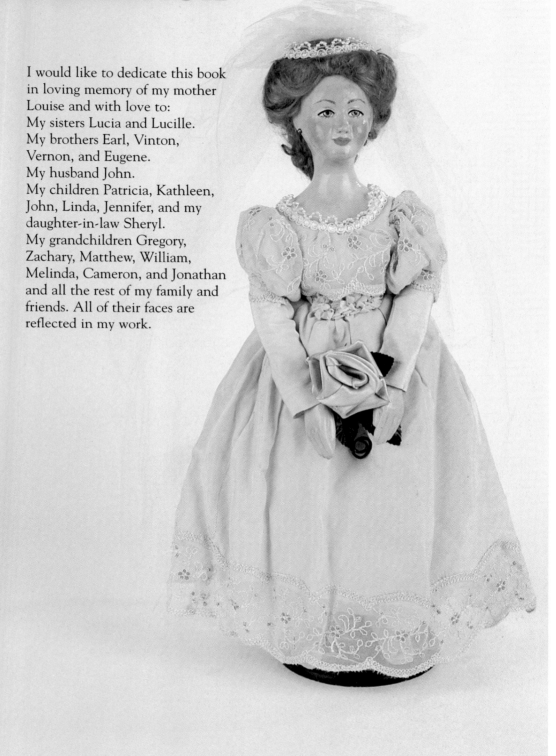

Table of Contents

PROJECTS

ntroduction

Beauty and the beast, children, and clowns all have one thing in common—they are just a few of the figures I've created since I began using papier mâché in the early 1970s.

The first dolls I made were Christmas gifts for my children. They were fashioned with big feet, funny hands, and short bodies. (They weren't meant to look that way but that's the way they turned out.) My children still have them and now we say they are "charming."

I have learned much more about sculpting since those first dolls, mainly through reading and experimentation. Many of the papier mâché figures I've made have received awards at arts and crafts and doll shows. I like to share my ideas and teach others what I've learned. While teaching classes in papier mâché, I discovered that many people want to be creative but have varying degrees of artistic ability and sewing skill and their questions prompted me to write this book. The ideas in this book are for these people. I try to keep sewing to a minimum and provide an artistic medium that can be as simple or artistic and expressive as each individual desires.

The seeds of my creativity were planted in childhood. I remember my mother reading aloud from her favorite book, *Grimm's Fairy Tales*. As a child, I was enchanted by fairy tales and even now, I love fairy and folk tales. Maybe I'm still a child inside and continue to dream as a child does. As a young mother, I read the stories to my children and now I read them to my grandchildren.

I love to make the characters from folk and fairy tales come alive in sculpture and as marionettes. I've never lost the wonderful feeling I had while listening to the enchanting stories and imagining all the beautiful scenery, marvelous characters, and fascinating happenings. In this book I hope to pass my wonder on to those who wish to pick up some papier mâché and sculpting tools and play for a while.

Doris Rockwell Gottilly

Getting Started

The projects in this book are made from either instant papier mâché or paper clay. You will learn the basic techniques to create figures using either product. I include complete how-to instructions, many photographs, and drawings to demonstrate how to make over 20 figures. The directions are easy to follow. After you've read the basic techniques and are comfortable with the basic steps, you'll be able to express your own individual style and creativity in the figures you make.

WHAT ARE PAPIER MÂCHÉ AND PAPER CLAY? ▪

Paper clay is ready to use when you purchase it. Instant papier mâché is mixed with water. These are just two of the manufacturers, there are others who make these products.

Papier mâché is a French term meaning "mashed paper." It was used in China and Japan long before European craftsmen began producing items from this paper mixture in the 16th century.

In the 18th century papier mâché factories produced all sorts of items, from vases to furniture. England, Russia, Italy, and Germany all manufactured papier mâché items during this period. The beautiful papier mâché dolls made during the 18th and 19th centuries have always fascinated me and have inspired many of my papier mâché dollmaking efforts.

Today's mashed paper is much refined and can be modeled and sculpted very much like sculptural clay. It is a very controllable medium to work with—if you make a mistake, you can easily correct it by adding more papier mâché or removing some. Papier mâché air dries, and when dry can be painted with any kind of paint. I prefer acrylic paints, so the instructions in the book call for acrylic paint products. Instant papier mâché comes in powder form, mixes easily with water, rolls out smooth, and can be used for any type of figure, from children to clowns.

Paper clay is a relatively new product and is wonderful to work with. It is clean, very easy to clean up, and allows for a great variety of sculpting possibilities. Paper clay is ready to use when you purchase it and is very smooth. This white modeling compound air dries to a hard finish, is odorless, non-toxic, non-greasy, mendable, and clings to all clean surfaces. It can be painted with any type of paint (I use acrylic paints and varnish). Paper clay is ideal for dolls, sculptures, miniatures and many other projects.

Both paper clay and instant papier mâché are economical because all mistakes are repairable (no throw-aways). If you don't like the first face you paint, let it dry, apply a light coat of gesso, and paint over it. Some of my figures have three or more faces over the first one (practice makes perfect). Another big advantage is that it air dries, so you don't need a kiln. You don't need a huge work space—just use a corner of your kitchen table, a few sculpting tools, a bowl of water, rolling pin, and plastic wrap, and you're ready to begin.

In any project, you can use either papier mâché or paper clay. Most often, the directions call for paper clay, but mâché will work too. It just depends on what you're comfortable with. I find paper clay a little easier to work with, since it requires no mixing and is always smooth. Keep in mind that in this book, the terms paper clay and papier mâché are interchangeable, and choose the medium you prefer.

I must confess that I much prefer today's paper clay and instant papier mâché over the old-fashioned torn newspaper soaked in warm water and mixed with wallpaper paste.

SUPPLY LIST ▪

Brushes ▪

A great variety of brushes are available. Look for brushes specifically for acrylic paints. Prices range from low to high and many brushes are sold in detail sets, round and flat sets, and most are inexpensive. These are available in art and craft stores and catalogs. Many brushes can also be found in hardware and home improvement stores.

I use mostly natural hair and bristle brushes, occasionally using nylon. I prefer brushes that apply a smooth coat of paint or varnish without leaving brush marks.

Never allow paint to dry on the brushes. Keep them in water while you're working. Before putting them away, wash them with soap and water and reshape them with your fingers.

The basic brush requirements are:
- 1/2″ or 3/4″-wide flat glaze soft hair brushes (1 for gesso, 1 for paint, 1 for varnish)
- 20/0 pointed nylon detail brush
- #6 nylon shader
- 3/0 liner brush (gold nylon) for fine lines around eyes
- cats tongue brush for eyes and lips
- lash and brow liner brush
- sable hair detail set:
  0, 1, 2, 3, 4, 6, 8
- brights for shading: 0, 2, 8, 12
- bristle brushes for gesso, painting, and varnishing large areas: #20 round, 2½″ flat, 1″ flat

Plastic sculpting tools ■

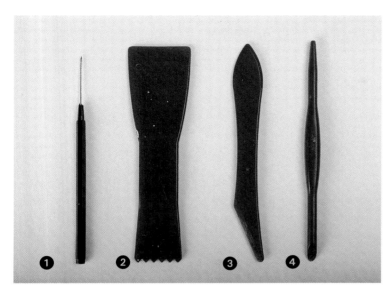

❶ Use the needlepoint tool to cut paper clay, pick up clay, and to add small pieces of paper clay, such as eyelids and coils for lips. Also used for detail work on the face, hands, and feet (especially the lines for fingers and toes).

❷ Use to smooth large sections of paper clay or make lines with the jagged end.

❸ Use to add on pieces of paper clay and to smooth them into paper clay. Use also to sculpt and add detail.

❹ Use the detail tool to press into paper clay around lips and eyes, to smooth, and to add detail. Use to shape eyelids, separate lips, and add dimples. Use the round end to make nostrils and shape eyes.

As you can see, modeling tools come in a variety of shapes and sizes—flats, curves, rounds, and detail. Each tool has two differently shaped ends. Many kitchen and household tools can also be used to sculpt and shape paper clay and papier mâché—rolling pin, garlic press, pizza roller, spoon, fork, knife, potato peeler, bamboo skewer, spatula, cuticle stick, etc.

Acrylic paints & varnishes ■

Many brands of artist quality acrylic paints and varnishes are available. I used Liquitex or Ceramcoat by Delta on the projects in this book. Whatever brand of acrylic paints you choose, test them on a piece of dry paper clay or papier mâché before using on your finished project.

Acrylic paints come in a variety of sizes, from 2 oz. to 8 oz. I usually buy 8 oz. bottles, but the 2 oz. size is more economical for beginners. Acrylic paints are premixes, can be thinned with water, and colors can be intermixed.

I recommend purchasing a few basic colors: white, black, red, flesh, dark flesh, dresden flesh, dark brown, green, light blue, and yellow. You can buy more colors as your work progresses and you need a greater variety of colors.

Before applying paint on dried paper clay or papier mâché, you'll need to seal it with gesso. Apply a smooth coat of gesso directly on the dry surface with a flat glaze brush. Gesso fills in rough spots as it seals. After the first coat is dry, apply a second coat.

After painting, you'll need to varnish your figure. I use acrylic polymer varnish. It's water-based, low odor, non-toxic, and cleans up with soap and water. It comes in satin with a medium sheen and matte with a flat finish. I most often use the satin finish, but the matte is good on faces when you don't want any shine.

The varnish forms a tough finish and dries clear and colorless. Stir it well and use a soft bristle flat brush to apply several thin coats, letting it dry completely between coats.

For larger figures, I use water-based polyurethane. It dries quickly and clear and is available in hardware and home improvement stores.

I often brush clear nail polish over painted eyes to add shine.

Sandpaper ■

You will need to sand some of the objects you make. Use fine to super fine grit on the faces and medium grit on larger items. Not much sanding is needed, so use a light touch. If you do a lot of sanding, wear a dust mask.

Miscellaneous ▪

Chances are, you already own much of what you'll need to complete a project. The list below is general, so refer to specific project instructions for special requirements. You may not need everything on the list for every project or you may need additional items.

❀ plastic wrap
❀ plastic bags
❀ small paring knife
❀ disposable gloves
❀ rubber bands
❀ rolling pin
❀ paper towels
❀ ruler and tape measure
❀ scissors
❀ small saw
❀ flexible plastic armature
❀ aluminum foil (12″-wide)
❀ Styrofoam balls or ovals
❀ crochet thread
❀ 18 gauge florist wire or 1/8″ plastic covered wire
❀ tacky white craft glue (dries clear)
❀ 2 6″ taper candles for arm armatures (1½″-2½″ in diameter)
❀ 2 7½″ taper candles for leg armatures (2″ - 3″ in diameter)
❀ cotton batting or polyester fiberfill

PREPARING THE PAPER CLAY OR PAPIER MÂCHÉ ▪

Because paper clay dries out when exposed to air, keep it in an air-tight plastic bag when you're not working with it. If the clay dries out, brush on some water and roll it in until the clay binds together and is flexible without breaking apart. Before beginning in earnest, play with a small amount, rolling it out, rolling it in your hands, making small shapes, adding water. This helps you get a feel for how to work with clay.

Slice off a 1/2″ strip, place it between two sheets of plastic wrap, and roll it out to the desired thickness (usually 1/4″ or 1/2″). Shape it as called for in the project instructions, let dry, sand if necessary, seal with gesso, and paint with acrylic paints. It hardens as it dries and the end result is lightweight and durable.

Instant papier mâché comes in powder form in grey or white and mixes easily with water. Mix in a plastic bag according to the manufacturer's instructions. Although it can be kept for days in the refrigerator, mix only as much as you need and use it within two days. Freshly mixed mâché sticks to the armature better. Roll it out between two sheets of plastic wrap to the required thickness.

DRYING ▪

Small paper clay items dry in a day or two, depending on room temperature and humidity. Larger items take longer, depending on the thickness of the clay. If cracks develop as the clay dries, rub moist clay into the crack and smooth it with your fingers.

Instant papier mâché may take longer to dry than paper clay, depending on how much water you add to the mâché. Drying times are affected by the thickness of the sculpture and room temperature and humidity. Most of the items in this book dried in three days at the ideal temperature of 75 degrees F or warmer. Be sure the item is completely dry before sealing it with gesso. The item is dry when it sounds like wood when tapped with a wood dowel.

SANDING ▪

When the papier mâché or paper clay is completely dry, sand off any bumps or lumps with medium to fine sandpaper (use only fine sandpaper on small heads). On most small heads, sanding is unnecessary because the clay dries super smooth. Paper clay can be sanded or carved like wood and any excess around the edges can be trimmed with scissors or a small saw.

Sanding paper clay is almost like sanding butter, so use a very light touch. Turn and check your progress as you work. Cut the sandpaper into small pieces and fold it into tiny triangles to get into the tiny spaces around the eyes and nose. You can use sanding to make small changes in the expression of the doll. Turn the head so you can see the features from all angles. If you sand too much don't worry, just add a small piece of clay, blend it in, and let it dry. Any mistake can be corrected by either adding clay or sanding it off.

Dollmaking Techniques

All figures are made using a few basic steps, which are fully explained in this book. The first step is to **create an armature**. Then **cover it** with paper clay or papier mâché. **Refine the features** by adding more clay or papier mâché or sanding some off. After the sculpture dries completely, **seal** with two coats of gesso. **Paint** and **varnish**, then **make and assemble the body. Add hair** and **dress** your figure in the costume of your choice.

MAKING AND COVERING AN ARMATURE ■

An armature is the skeleton of your project and should be simple and sturdy. If you make your own armature you can create your own shape and sculpture. You can buy flexible plastic body armatures or make wire armatures in body shapes or use something as basic as a soda bottle as an armature (the rabbit on page 104 is made over a soda bottle).

There are two ways to make a head armature, one with the head and neck, and the other with the head, neck, and bodice. Above are the materials used to make a head/neck/bodice armature and arm and leg armatures— Styrofoam shapes, aluminum foil, scissors, taper candles, tape measure. The head/neck/bodice parts are sculpted around a Styrofoam oval or ball wrapped in aluminum foil and covered with paper clay or papier mâché. Legs and arms are made by wrapping aluminum foil around taper candles to form an armature. The candles are removed when the legs and arms are complete. To create a head/neck/bodice, fold aluminum foil around a Styrofoam egg and twist the foil to form a neck. Spread out the foil and fold it up and under to shape the bodice. If you have too much aluminum foil, trim it with scissors.

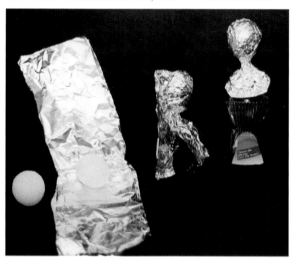

Place the Styrofoam ball in the center of a 4˝ x 11˝ piece of foil as shown above, fold the foil over and shape, twist, and smooth each side of the head. Form a neck with the foil at the base. Hold the foil ball in one hand and twist the foil the other way to shape the neck. Rough in the facial features by twisting and squeezing the foil to shape the eye sockets, nose, and chin. Use a detergent bottle to support the head while you shape the bodice with foil. Fold about 2˝ foil under as you shape.

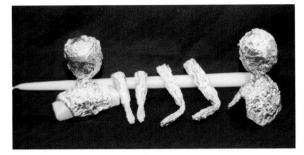

Here are armatures of two heads/bodices and armatures of arms and legs resting on the candles that were used to shape them. The candles are removed when the pieces are dry. Candles can be used over again for another project.

Arm and leg armature with candles inserted. Notice how the foot is shaped. Candles remain inside until the paper clay or mâché has been applied over the armature.

Paper clay, sculpting tool set, rolling pin, a bowl of water, and four head armatures. All ready to begin sculpting.

Use 1/2 lb. of paper clay to cover a 3″ Styrofoam oval wrapped in aluminum foil and to create the lower arms and legs. Place a piece of plastic wrap on the table and keep more plastic wrap handy. You'll need a bowl of water, paper towels, a rolling pin, a set of four sculpting tools, paint brushes, and a plastic bag to hold unused paper clay so it won't dry out. The clay dries quickly when exposed to air. Slice the paper clay into 1/4″ slices with a small knife. Place a piece of plastic over the clay so it's sandwiched between two pieces of plastic.

Two armatures. The one on the left is made with a round Styrofoam ball and the one on the right is made with an oval. Each has a bodice. The oval one is resting on a piece of Styrofoam cut out to use as a support while sculpting.

Use a rolling pin to flatten the clay until all the strips are blended into one piece 1/4″ thick. Place the head armature on the clay and trace around the head with a needlepoint sculpting tool. Make the circle about 1/2″ wider than the armature. Do this twice, so you'll have one piece for the front and one for the back.

Cut out the front piece of paper clay and carefully pick it up. It feels and looks like pie crust.

Carefully drape the paper clay piece over the front of the armature with the narrow area pressed in at the neck. Press upward over the face, up to the top of the head. Use your thumb and fingers to press the clay firmly on the head and push down. Dip your fingers in water from time to time and smooth and blend the clay with your thumb until it sticks to each side of the head. The paper clay will smooth out beautifully.

Pick up the back piece of clay and place it on the back of the head armature. Begin pressing at the neck and work upward. Dip the sculpting tool in water and ease paper clay over the side seam and smooth and blend up the right side of the head. This armature has only the head and neck, no bodice.

Continue smoothing the clay with the sculpting tool. Notice which tool is used for smoothing and my hand position while I work.

Dip the tool in water again and smooth and blend the paper clay, working from the bottom upward. The seams are looking good. The front pieces are all blended as one piece. Turn the head as you work, checking from all angles.

Dip your fingers in water and continue to smooth the clay until it's completely smooth. You'll find that your thumb is one of your most important "sculpting tools." Clean the sculpting tools in soapy water and dry them with a paper towel.

Place a piece of black string on the head and mark the horizontal center of the face so you can plan the placement of the eyes, nose, mouth, and ears. Pull the string taut so it makes a line across the center of the face. Move the string up to where you want to place the eyes and make another string line.

Place the string on the head and mark the vertical center of the face. This will help you place the mouth, nose, eyes, and eyebrows.

FACIAL ADD-ONS ▮

You'll use add-on pieces of clay for the eyes, nose, lips, chin, cheeks, forehead, and ears. Cut small circular or oval shapes from the 1/4˝ thick clay (individual project directions give specific add-on requirements). This is an easy technique for crafters new to sculpting.

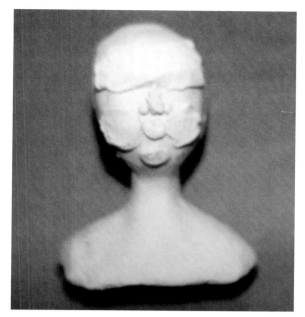

Head showing the add-ons for the forehead, nose, cheeks, lips, and chin.

Use the needlepoint tool to carefully pick up the eyes and place them on the face. Then add the nose, mouth, and chin pieces. Use the flat end of the detail tool to smooth and blend the add-ons to the face, working from the outer edge of the add-on.

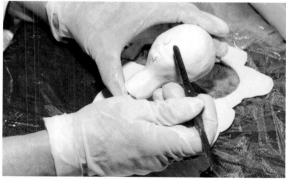

Brush on a little water (very little) as you continue to smooth the features. I am using the

detail tool to smooth the eyes, nose, and mouth.

Continue to smooth and sculpt. Note the position of the sculpting tool and the way it's held. Blend clay around the nose and the lips (note my hand position).

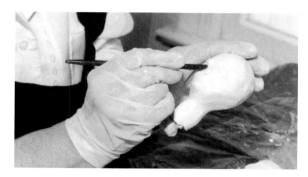

Smooth the clay around the eyes and define eyelids with the flat end of the detail tool (note my hand position). The small sculpting tool is held like a pencil and works great for detail work around eyes and lips.

Cut out two small circles for cheeks. Blend and smooth them into the face. I use the side of the sculpting tool to blend in and smooth the cheeks upward toward the side of the head.

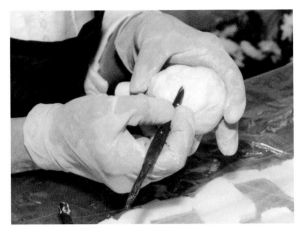

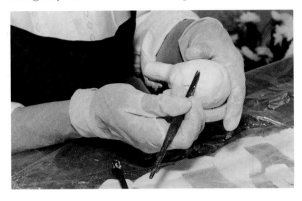

Use a small detail brush dipped in water to sculpt and blend clay around the lips. Use the round end of the detail tool to add dimples by pressing in lightly on each side of the lips and in the chin.

Work on the eyes, shaping and blending the clay down on each side and inward at the nose. Note how to hold the head and how the sculpting tools are held and used. Push in firmly with your thumbs to form small indentations on each side of the nose. Smooth the clay out towards the temples. Continue blending the cutouts with the round end sculpting tool. Turn the head as you work so you can see how the sculpture is developing from all angles. Use your thumbs to push clay up on the cheeks and push in on each side near the temples to make a very slight indentation.

Change sculpting tools and work on detail and the smoothness of the features. If you're tired or getting frustrated, take a break for a few minutes. Cover the head with plastic to keep the paper clay from drying out.

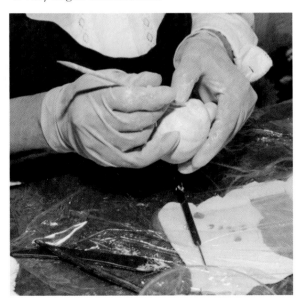

Use a cuticle stick to shape the eyelids by blending in a small coil of clay over each eye. Add coils for the lips and blend in and shape with the cuticle stick. Part the center of the lips, gently pushing up for the top lip and down for the bottom lip. Brush a tiny bit of water on the clay from time to time to keep the clay from drying out.

Head showing the add-ons blended and smoothed to form recognizable facial features.

The ears have been added and the features refined. When it's completely dry, this head can be carefully sanded.

BASIC SHAPES FOR FACIAL FEATURES ▪

basic nose shape

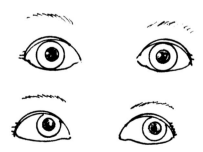

basic eye shapes

basic lips formed from rolled coils

basic ear shape

CHILDREN'S FACIAL FEATURES ▪

placement of eyes, nose, and mouth for children. Eyes are halfway down from the top of the head.

all shapes on a baby are round

To make cheeks for children or any other head extra round, add extra small circles of paper clay under larger circle add-ons. Add the small piece first and blend into the paper clay covered armature, then add the second piece and smooth it in. For extra-round cheeks, add a third circle of clay and smooth it in. This will make the cheeks nice and round.

SANDING ▪

Use super fine sandpaper cut in small pieces. Paper clay sands *very easily* so be careful you don't sand off the detail or facial features.

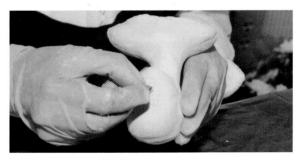

Fold sandpaper into tiny triangles to get into hard-to-reach places around the eyes, nose, and mouth.

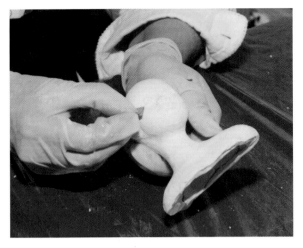

Turn the head as you sand it. It's important to look at the features from all angles.

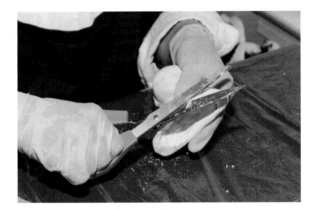

Trim off excess clay with scissors.

Excess clay can also be scraped off with a knife. Always carve away from your body.

Remove the aluminum foil inside the bodice with small needle nose pliers. Seal with two coats of gesso and let dry.

MAKING ARMS AND LEGS

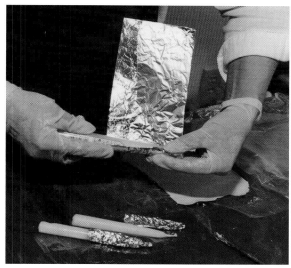

Wrap and shape aluminum foil around the tapered end of two 7½˝ candles to shape the leg armatures. Use two 6˝ candles for the arm shapes. The candles are removed when the paper clay has dried.

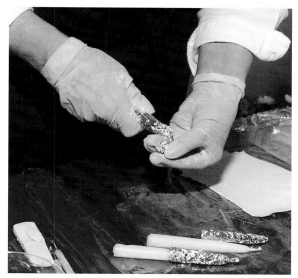

Roll several layers of aluminum foil around each candle and squeeze and shape as you wrap. For the arms, pull about 1˝ of foil off the candle at the tapered end and squeeze it with your thumb and index finger to shape a wrist and a small shovel hand. For the legs, carefully pull about 1½˝ foil off each candle and bend it upward to shape the foot. Leave the foil on the candles.

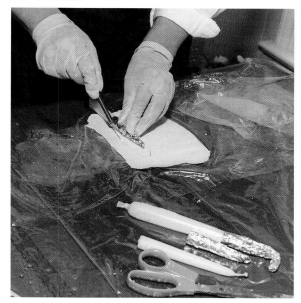

Roll out the paper clay to a thickness of 1/4˝. Place one of the armatures on the paper clay and trace around it, adding about 1/2˝ all the way around. Use a needlepoint tool dipped in water to cut the paper clay. Cut out one shape at a time and work with it until that piece is finished. Here I'm cutting out the shape for an arm.

Carefully pick up the paper clay cutout with the needlepoint tool. Notice the position of my hands as I work.

Drape the paper clay cutout for an arm over the armature and press and wrap paper clay around it with the clay seam in back. Dip your fingers in water and pinch and smooth the clay until the seams are blended and smooth. Shape a shovel type hand (a cupped hand with no fingers, just a small thumb added) on the end of each arm.

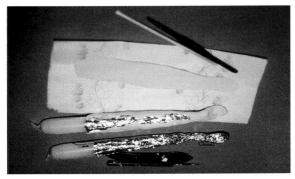

A closer look at the right arm half covered with paper clay. Notice the hand shape. The clay

cutout on the paper towel will cover the rest of this arm. There are three basic styles of hands: the small shovel hand which is an oval shape with a small thumb added; the closed finger hand with fingers suggested with a needlepoint tool; and the shaped and sculpted hand with the fingers separated.

With a needle tool, trim excess paper clay from the top of the arm. When making the arms, be sure to make a left one and a right one. The hands will probably cup in towards the body. Add more clay to fill in, cut out small pieces and smooth them into the hand. Set aside to dry and start another piece. When all the pieces are dry, they are ready to be sanded, sealed with gesso, and painted.

The right arm has been finished and the paper clay has been cut out for the left arm. Notice the shape of the cutout. Wrap the cutout around the armature with the seam on the underside.

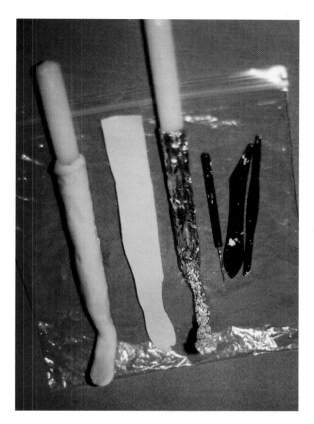

One leg has been completely covered with clay. Notice the small coil of clay that's been added to the top of the leg section to form a rim. This rim will later help secure the cloth part of the leg.

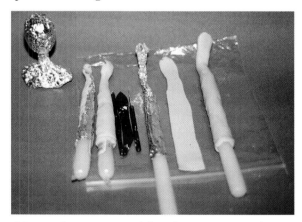

Here's the uncovered head armature with one of the arm armatures (top 4″ of candle wrapped with foil) half covered with paper clay and the other fully covered. To the right of the sculpting tools is a leg armature with no paper clay and the paper clay cutout that will cover it. The leg on the far right is completely covered. Remove the candles after the paper clay dries.

ADDING HAIR ▪

There are a variety of hair styles on the figures in this book. Techniques include sculpting hair from papier mâché, using imprinted paper clay, pressing clay through a garlic press, or using angora, mohair, crochet thread, or mini curls to make hair. Of course, there are wonderful wigs available as well as packaged hair in strands that can be cut to length and glued on.

Garlic press hair ▪

Place a piece of paper clay in a garlic press and squeeze. The assorted lengths of clay strands can be used to create hair. I used garlic press strands to make the hair on the baby doll.

Separate the strands of paper clay and curl and press them to the paper clay head. This photo shows the finished results after the clay has dried, sealed with gesso, sanded, then painted.

The back of the baby doll head is a good example of garlic press hair.

Imprinted paper clay hair ◼

To imprint on clay, roll out the clay to 1/4″ thick and place lace or any flat textured object or pattern on the clay. Roll the pattern into the clay with a rolling pin. In these photos, I used crochet thread wrapped around a piece of cardboard to make the imprint. All sorts of trims make lovely patterns when pressed into paper clay and can be used to decorate legs, shoes, bodices, or hair. Let your imagination go wild—all sorts of designs are possible.

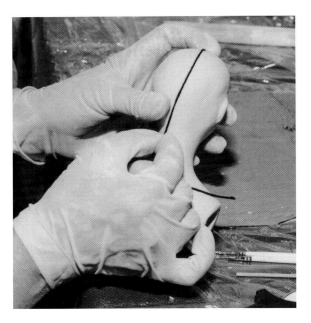

Measure the back of the head with a string to determine what length piece of paper clay you'll need. Decide on a style before cutting the clay and draw a sketch of the style.

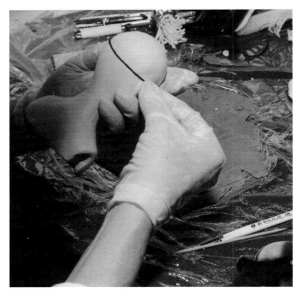

Measure across the head for the width of the head, then transfer the measurements to the paper clay.

I imprinted a "hair design" on this paper clay with a 2½″ x 3″ piece of cardboard wrapped with crochet thread. Roll out the clay about 1/4″ thick, place the cardboard on the clay and press it in with a rolling pin. Cut a piece of clay large enough to cover the head. I used a pizza cutter to cut the paper clay, but you can also use a needlepoint tool.

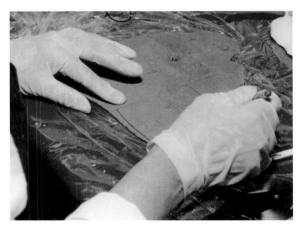

Carefully pick up the clay for the back of the head. Use a paint brush to dampen the back of the doll's head with a little bit of water. I'm using a head that has already been dried, sealed with gesso, and painted with flesh tone, but you

can add hair before sealing and painting if you wish.

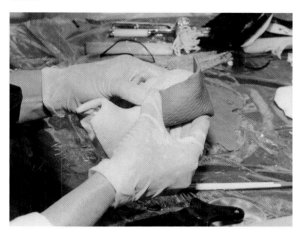

Carefully place the paper clay on the back of the head and press it to the head with your fingers.

When pressing the clay onto the head, be careful not to smooth out the imprinted lines.

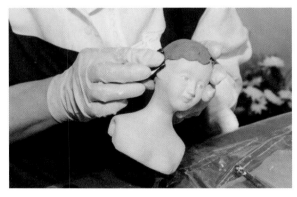

Use a small piece of cardboard wrapped with crochet thread to press paper clay hair to the head. The crochet thread keeps the imprinted lines intact.

Brush water on the edges of the clay to keep it moist while you work.

If you want to add curls, cut strips of clay with a pizza cutter.

Wrap clay strips around a wet bamboo skewer to shape a long curl. Start from the bottom of the skewer and wrap upward. Carefully slide the

curl off the skewer. You can make smaller curls with a narrower strip of clay wrapped around a needle tool.

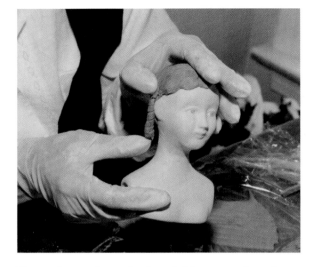

Place the curl on the head. Use your thumb to gently hold the top of the curl as you press it in place.

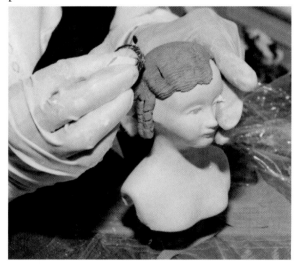

Press the curls into the hair and use a small piece of cardboard wrapped with crochet thread to crimp waves into the clay.

Samples of crochet thread imprinted clay hair. Hansel and Gretal are marionettes I made a few years ago with hair made with the imprinting technique.

I'm using a potato peeler to shave off small pieces of paper clay to use for a small rose. Paper clay is wonderfully easy to cut, slice, roll, and shape.

Making a mohair wig

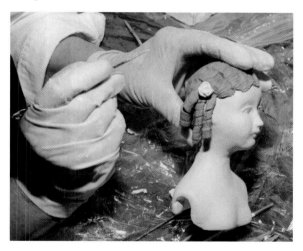

Here the small rose has been placed above the curls. When all the curls are dry, seal with gesso.

To make a mohair wig, you'll need the mohair, thread to match, wax paper, super-tacky glue, and a sewing machine. These instructions work with curly crepe wool and polypropylene filament strands also.

❶ Measure from the top center to the side of the head and double that number. Cut the mohair wide enough to fit from the center forehead to the back of the head and as long as you want the hairstyle to be. For fuller hair, cut two pieces and layer them on the head.

2 Place the mohair between two pieces of wax paper and sew a seam down the center on the sewing machine. This seam becomes the center part. The wax paper keeps the mohair from getting tangled in the bobbin case. After sewing the seam, remove the wax paper.

3 Cut a piece for the bangs. Bangs can be short, long, or the same length as the rest of the hair. They can fall over the forehead or be pulled back to cover the center seam and styled in with the rest of the hair.

4 Brush glue on the top and sides of the finished head. Glue the bang section first, then the main section. Secure the hair in place with rubber bands and let dry. If adding a second layer, let the bottom layer dry completely, then apply glue to the center seam and place the top layer on top. Secure with rubber bands and let dry. When the glue has dried, the hair can be trimmed, styled with curls, braided, left straight, or whatever you desire. Do not comb the mohair, as it will pull out. I use a hair prong or needle to fluff up and separate a few strands to curl.

5 To make add-on curls, wrap a strand of mohair around a large needle, paint brush, or pencil, depending on the size curl you want. Lightly spray the curl with hair spray. Make all the curls before gluing them to the wig.

6 After all curls are made and the glue has dried, gently style the hair and tie on ribbons or other decorative trims.

Mini curls

You can purchase hair in individual strands or curls, which makes for an easy way to create the curly-headed look.

1 Cut curls twice the length you want them, then fold them in half.

2 Apply dots of glue to the head and glue on the curls (fold at the head). Hold firmly until the glue sets. Work from the back neckline up toward the forehead, then from each side up to the center. Repeat until you're pleased with the fullness.

3 After all the pieces are securely glued to the head, brush and style with a hair prong and trim if necessary.

CONSTRUCTING THE CLOTH BODY

Make the cloth body using the pattern for whatever doll you're making. For every figure in this book, you'll find a pattern with basic sewing instructions. I often use unbleached muslin for the body because it's easy to work with and is readily available.

You'll need a sewing machine, thread to match the fabrics, scissors, straight pins, tape measure, pencil, needles for hand sewing, 5″ needle for assembling and sewing arms and legs to the cloth bodies, small snaps or Velcro snaps, elastic 1/8″ wide, cotton or polyester stuffing, heavy duty thread, an assortment of trims, laces, bells, and ribbons 1/4″ wide.

Use the straight stitch on your sewing machine to sew all seams. You can sew by hand if you don't have a machine. Press the seams before proceeding to the next step in sewing. Sew up the neck and back openings with neat slip stitches. Use heavy duty thread to attach arms and legs to the body. The fabric required for the cloth bodies is either 1/4 or 1/2 yard.

Measure the paper clay arms and legs and adjust the size of the arm openings on the pattern to fit. Sew the darts in the back and front. Start on the left side and sew from the leg, up the side, under the arm. Sew up the right side. Leave openings for the paper clay arms and legs. Leave an opening at the neck for turning the body and stuffing. Turn the body right side out and hem the openings.

Attach the cloth arms and legs to the cloth body with a piece of heavy duty upholstery or button thread. Tie the thread in a knot on each arm and leg. Go from right to left and knot.

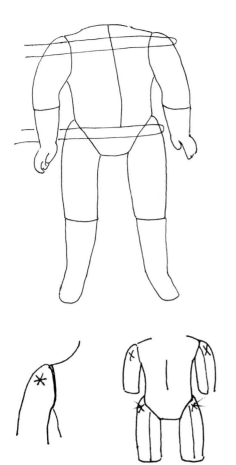

Repeat the procedure from left to right and tie and knot. I put a drop of glue on each knot to make them more secure. Hem the arm and leg openings before gluing in the paper clay arms and legs. Shown is an example of the body used for the 15″ child, Polcinella, Jingles, and the baby doll.

Making accessories ▪

Shoes ▪

You can make shoes from rolled out paper clay. Cover the cloth foot with plastic wrap held in place with a rubber band.

To add texture, imprint the clay with a mesh bag before cutting out the shape of the shoe.

Cut out one shoe pattern for the right side of the foot and press it over the foot. These are the wooden-look shoes made for Polcinella. Shape the clay with your fingers until it molds to the foot with the seam on the bottom. Add more clay as needed.

Cut out the other side of the shoe and press it to the foot, overlapping at the seam and pinching the clay together. Let the shoe dry on the foot overnight. Remove the shoe and sand if necessary, then varnish it. After the varnish is dry, remove the plastic wrap from the foot and put the shoe on.

Hat

This simple hat is made with clay that's been imprinted with a crocheted doily. The intricate pattern of the doily on the clay makes a pretty design. Cut out the clay doily, place it on the head, and shape it to fit. Wrap the head with plastic wrap before fitting the hat, so the two pieces don't stick together. Let the clay hat dry on the head. When dry, remove it and paint or decorate it as desired.

TIPS AND ALTERNATIVES

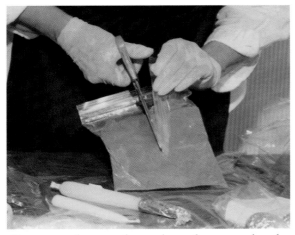

You can change the color of paper clay by brushing acrylic paint over moist paper clay and

kneading it to blend in the color. Store the colored clay in a plastic bag to keep it from drying out.

To make an imprint on clay, first roll it to 1/4˝ thick. Here I'm using a piece of cardboard wrapped with crochet thread which has been glued on. This will make the imprint of fine lines on the clay. Use a rolling pin to press the card into the clay. This lined clay will be used for hair.

Paper clay over an existing object

Many items can be used as a base for a paper clay sculpture. You can leave the clay on the piece or remove it after it's dried.

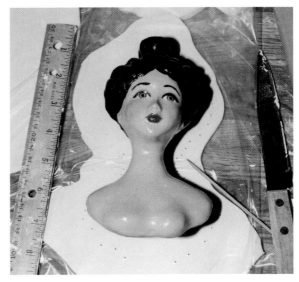

For example, I used one of my original porcelain heads (Adelaide) as the basis for this sculpture. Brush the head with petroleum jelly to keep the clay from sticking. Roll out the clay to 1/4″-1/2″ and cut out the outline of the head. Use 1/4″ thick clay over the face, 1/2″ over the neck, bodice, and hair. (Many broken items can be covered permanently with maché or paper clay, painted, and used again.)

Drape the paper clay over the head and cut off the excess. Press the clay to the shape of the doll's face and hair. Do this with two separate pieces of clay, one for the front and one for the back, but don't join the two pieces, keep a small gap between them. After the clay dries completely, remove the pieces from the model.

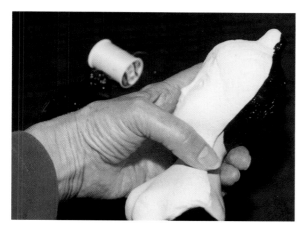

A side view of the dried clay. Notice how the nose and mouth detail has been shaped. You can add extra pieces if you want to make the nose larger or enhance any feature.

The new piece is fragile because it is only 1/4″-1/2″ thick and hollow.

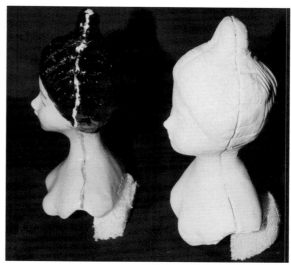

You can see the line on the porcelain head that separated the two paper clay pieces. Join the front and back pieces together at the seamline with a strip of paper clay along the seam. Let it dry and reinforce the seam by adding more paper clay on the inside of the bodice and up to the neck. After the head is thoroughly dry, sand the seamline. Check to see if additional work is needed on the face or bodice. When dry, seal with two coats of gesso and lightly sand. To seal and strengthen the head and bodice, pour gesso inside the head, then pour it out. The head is now ready to paint and varnish.

Pressed paper clay in a plaster mold ■

I use my original two part molds that I'm no longer using for porcelain as molds for paper clay. Once you've used the molds with paper clay or papier mâché, they are no longer suitable for porcelain.

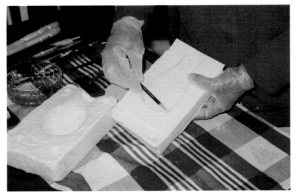

Make patterns by placing paper over the mold shapes and rubbing the edges with a pencil. Cut out the patterns, adding 1″ all around. Roll out the paper clay to 1/2″ thick. Place the pattern on the paper clay and cut it out.

Line the molds with plastic wrap, extending the wrap over the sides of the mold. If you prefer, you can shake talc into the molds instead of lining them with plastic wrap. If using talc, make sure the entire mold surface is covered, then tap out the excess. Press the paper clay firmly into the mold, pushing it into all the indentations.

Roll small pieces of paper clay into balls about the size of a marble and push them firmly into the crevices of the mold, making sure all the detail is picked up. You may need to do this for the nose, eyes, and lips. The extra paper clay supports the eyes, nose, and mouth.

Cut 1/2″ wide strips of paper clay and push them in all around the edge of the mold.

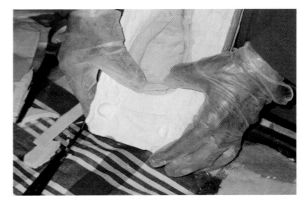

Trim off any clay that overlaps the seamline of the mold. Repeat this process for all the molds, then let the filled molds dry for two days. The paper clay should come out easily when dry. When the clay has dried, carefully remove it from the mold by lifting out the plastic wrap. (If you used talc, tip the molds over and tap until the pieces come out.) If the plastic wrap made lines in the paper clay, wet your fingers and rub some clay over the lines. Let dry and lightly sand with fine sandpaper. Glue the front and back half of the paper clay sculpture together at the seamlines. When the glue has dried, add extra paper clay to any rough spots along the seamline. Let the clay dry and sand along the seamlines until smooth.

Results from the press mold technique. These are pieces for Victoria, the 20″ lady doll. You may need to do additional work on the eyes, nose, and mouth after the head is removed from the plaster mold. If the features did not press in completely, cut small pieces of thin paper clay and add it on the tip of the nose or lips as needed. Let the clay dry and lightly sand. You can add lines between fingers and toes or separate them with the needlepoint tool. Seal with two coats of gesso and paint as desired. To see how beautifully this technique turns out, see Victoria on the Dedication page.

PAINTING ■

Here's a two-part mold for hands and lower arms.

Apply two coats of flesh paint to the head and bodice. Let each coat dry completely. Use a detail brush to paint on the eyebrows and eyelids.

Add subtle cheek color by rubbing in creme rouge make-up with a cotton swab. Use the swab to blend in the rouge so there's no distinct line of color. Add more color if necessary and blend it in. I generally use copper, bronze, coral, or peach creme rouge make-up. You can also use acrylic paint to rouge cheeks. Mix pink or peach with flesh paint for ladies and children. Notice my hand position.

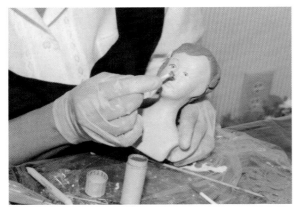

Add a tiny bit of rouge to the nose. Notice how each detail makes the face come alive.

Brushing color on the lips. I chose a light peach acrylic paint for the lips on this doll. When you've finished painting, coat with two or more coats of varnish.

TURNING DOLLS INTO SCULPTURES ■

Use a wood base to fit the figure size. Just make sure it's large and stable enough to hold the figure(s) without tipping over. For the Harlequin and 17″-22″ figures, I used a block 6″ x 8″ x 1″ with a 7/16″ dowel. For Kate and Keisha and 12″-15″ figures, I used a block 6″ x 9″ x 3/4″ with a 1/4″-1/2″ dowel. Cut the dowel to fit the height of the figure.

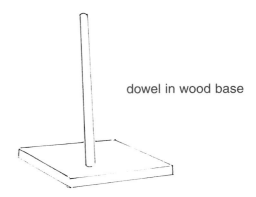

dowel in wood base

Drill a hole in the center of a wood base and glue a dowel in the hole.

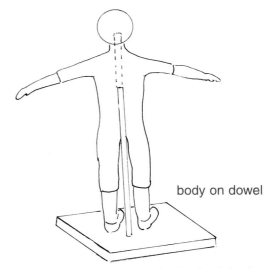

body on dowel

Cut a 1″ vertical opening in the back of the figure above the waistline. Slide the wooden dowel in the opening and push it upward into the doll's neck. Push stuffing into the upper part of the body, around the neck and shoulders. Continue to stuff small pieces into the front and then the back to the waist. Stuff the bottom half of the body firmly from the waist down to the legs.

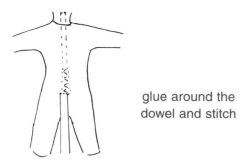

glue around the
dowel and stitch

Put glue around the wood dowel and stitch up
the opening.

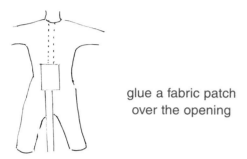

glue a fabric patch
over the opening

Glue a piece of body fabric 2″ x 3″ over the
sewn opening in the back. Let the glue dry.
Brush the entire body with a coat of acrylic varnish. Let dry, and brush on a second coat of varnish.

Now you can add the wig and the costume.
There are two ways to finish the costume. The
first is to make the costume from cloth and put
it on the figure. It can be left as is or coated
with acrylic varnish. An alternative is to make
the costume from fine art tissue paper and
assemble and glue it to the figure. Paper can
have designs painted on with acrylic paints and
then varnished. The art figures can be used as
decorative sculptures. The wood base can be
varnished or painted to complement the costume. Kate and Keisha were made in this way
with fine art tissue for their costumes.

MAKING MINIATURES

All the figures and dolls in this book can be
made into miniatures by reducing the patterns
for the bodies and costumes by one half.
Reduce the size of the armatures and Styrofoam
balls and ovals and the size of the candles used
to form the armatures for the arms and the legs
by one half.

Making miniatures of all the figures reduces
the cost of making each figure and allows you to
display them in less space.

SAVING RECYCLABLES

Save cardboard boxes, plastic bottles, cere-
al boxes, cardboard tubes from wax paper and
paper towels, all sorts of plastic containers
with lids, paper bags, and any item that can
be used to form and shape an armature. All
sizes and shapes can be used. Your imagination can guide you on how to use the items in
your recycle bin.

Plastic containers (small, medium, and
large) are useful as water and paint containers.
Jars are handy for rinsing brushes and storing
paints.

Paper bags can be torn into strips of various
widths from 1/2″ up and soaked in water then
dipped in glue and used to strengthen armatures
before covering with papier mâché. The length
of each strip depends on the size of the sculpture you are making. Practice with pieces torn
1″ x 8″ and overlap each strip about 1/4″. Cover
the entire form with this technique. Designs
can be made as you overlap and weave each
strip. This technique can be used by itself and
then sealed with gesso and painted.

All sorts of sculptures can be made with
boxes and paper bags used as papier mâché—
doll houses, miniature Christmas villages, cars,
abstract designs of any color and shape.

KEEPING A REFERENCE FILE

It is necessary to have all sorts of reference
material at your fingertips when you are creat-
ing these figures. Over the years I have kept a
reference file of ideas, photos, and pictures on
all sorts of things that interest me. All types
of fashions, faces, expressions, accessories—
anything from the past to the present that I
might need while I am working. I catalog
each one according to subject and file them in
a photo album. I add to the file and delete at
times and I always have a ready supply of
ideas and reference material when I need it in
a hurry.

Projects

Read the techniques section for general instructions, then adapt them to the individual project. In addition to the materials listed, you'll need tools, brushes, gesso, glue, and paper, paints, varnish, and costumes.

22" CINDY FASHION DOLL

MATERIALS

paper clay or papier mâché
flexible plastic armature
    (Dollspart #050183)
3˝ Styrofoam oval for head armature
aluminum foil
2 taper candles for leg armatures
2 taper candles for arm armatures
Dynel wig
fabric and stuffing for cloth body (Cindy cloth
    body pattern on page 117)
dress for 20˝-22˝ figure (pattern on page 142)

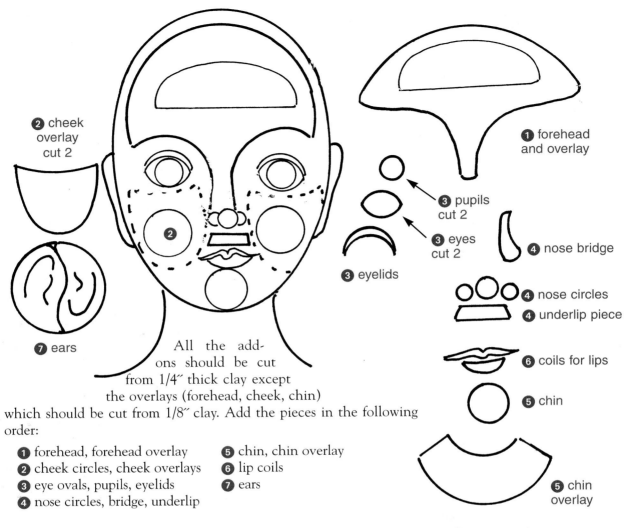

2 cheek overlay cut 2

1 forehead and overlay

3 pupils cut 2

3 eyes cut 2

3 eyelids

4 nose bridge

4 nose circles

4 underlip piece

6 coils for lips

5 chin

7 ears

5 chin overlay

All the add-ons should be cut from 1/4″ thick clay except the overlays (forehead, cheek, chin) which should be cut from 1/8″ clay. Add the pieces in the following order:

1 forehead, forehead overlay
2 cheek circles, cheek overlays
3 eye ovals, pupils, eyelids
4 nose circles, bridge, underlip
5 chin, chin overlay
6 lip coils
7 ears

The Styrofoam oval has been covered with foil and a bodice formed as described in the Techniques section. Trace the outline on paper clay and cut out the shape with a needlepoint tool. Store excess paper clay in a plastic bag.

The side view of Cindy's head covered with 1/4″ layer of paper clay. Notice how smooth the paper clay is on the front of the face and bodice.

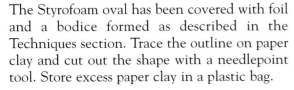

The first coat of flesh paint has been applied. When the first coat is dry, apply a second coat.

Paper clay has been added to the back of the head and extra pieces added for the forehead, nose, lips, ears, and sculpted and smoothed. My Cindy doll has painted eyes, but in this photo I've inserted plastic eyes (10mm oval) to show you how it's done. After sculpting and smoothing the facial features and ears, set in the eyes. Check to see if they are the proper depth. If they look like they are ready to pop out, take them out and remove some clay behind them. When they look good, roll two small coils and press one across the top of each eye to form the upper eyelid. Add two more small coils for the lower lids. The coils are very small, 1/8″ thick and 7/8″ wide. Use a tiny detail brush to pick them up and place them under the eyes.

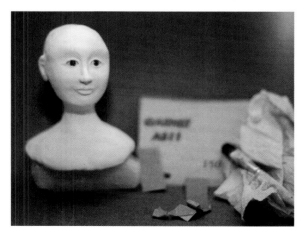

Cindy's head has been lightly sanded. Brush on two coats of gesso.

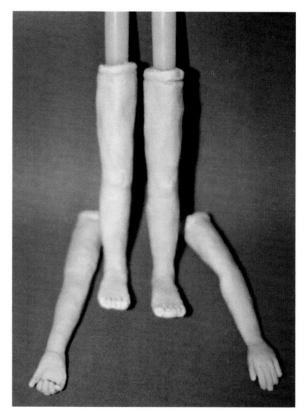

Completed sculptures of paper clay arms and legs over candle and foil armatures. Remember to size the leg and arm openings to fit the plastic armature. Test the armature opening over the plastic body armature before covering with paper clay.

Cindy's arms and legs, actual size. When sculpting the arms and legs, remember to make a left and right of each. The left hand has fingers and a thumb, the right hand has fingers folded. Add on a coil thumb. The fingers were folded over a paint brush handle as I sculpted. I used a needlepoint tool and a small detail brush to shape and separate the fingers. Remember to size the openings to fit the plastic poseable body armature. Try the foil armature opening over the plastic armature before covering it with paper clay.

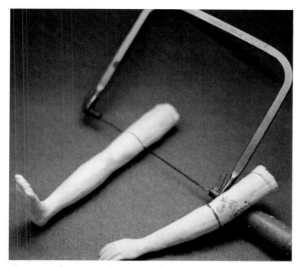

Paper clay can be sawed easily when dried. I made the arms and legs much too long, so I cut them to the required length. Lightly sand and paint flesh. For easy painting, place the arms and legs on skewers or dowels inserted into Styrofoam.

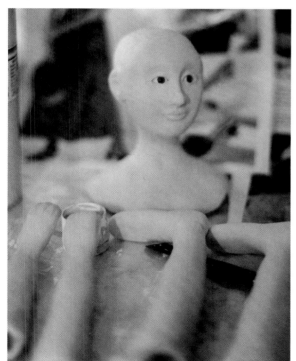

Cindy's head, arms, and legs have been painted flesh. Measure around the head above the ears for wig size.

Paint the facial details now—lips, cheeks, eyelids, and eyebrows. I mixed red with flesh tone paint for the lips, lined the eyelids with black, and brushed on bronze creme rouge then gently wiped off the excess with a piece of cotton. This photo shows the head with the wig on, but the facial painting should be done before the wig is added. After all the paint is dry, use a 1/2″ flat glaze brush to carefully apply two thin coats of acrylic satin varnish, letting the first dry before applying the second. Brush on the varnish smoothly, with minimum brush strokes.

I glued a curly 9″ Dynel wig to the varnished head. The flexible plastic armature inside the cloth body allows the doll to be poised in many ways. The paper clay head/bodice, arms, and legs are finished and ready to be assembled.

Sew the cloth body pattern pieces together and put it over the flexible plastic armature to make sure it fits. Leave notches of the plastic armature extended to later slide into the paper clay arms and legs.

Remove the plastic armature from the cloth body. Wrap the plastic armature with strips of cotton batting and tie them on with thread. Slide the armature through the large neck opening in the cloth body, feet first with arms up. Add more stuffing around the plastic armature. Put some glue inside the paper clay arms and slide them over the two arm notches of the plastic armature. Repeat with the paper clay legs. Put glue on the inside of the cloth arms and legs and pull each cloth arm and leg down over the paper clay arms and legs tie with thread. When the glue is dry, stuff the body firmly at the bodice and hand-stitch the opening across the bodice/neck. Glue the head/bodice to the body. Apply glue to the underside of the bodice and place it over the top of the body, as shown in the photograph. Use two rubber bands to hold the head to the body until the glue dries. Remove the rubber bands.

12"
BABY DOLL

MATERIALS

paper clay or papier mâché
3″ round Styrofoam ball for head armature
aluminum foil (4″ x 9″)
10mm plastic eyes
1/4 yard peach chintz fabric for cloth body
    (12″ baby cloth body pattern on page 118)
stuffing for body
costume

Think round when sculpting children. Watch the proportions so they will look like babies. The distance between the eyes should be the width of the eye. The ears should be small and line up with the top of the eye and the end of the nose. The neck will be very short, the head seems to fall right into the chest. The shoulders should be small, and the face should have a high forehead and round chubby cheeks. On the hands, the fingers are closed with the thumb wrapped around the fingers. Add dimples on the hands. Keep it simple. Remember, this is a doll, not a portrait.

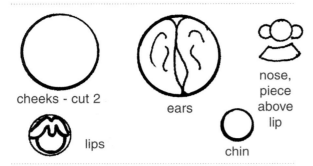

cheeks - cut 2

ears

nose, piece above lip

lips

chin

Cover the head armature with clay and add on the extra pieces for the cheeks, chin, lips, nose, and ears. Use the sculpting tools to blend in and smooth the clay. Press in around the nose and lips and add detail in the nostrils and eyelids. Open the lips for a smile. Practice setting in the 10mm plastic eyes until they look right.

The baby doll head armature half covered with paper clay. The cutout for the back section is ready for application. I picked up the paper clay with my fingers and pressed it firmly on the armature.

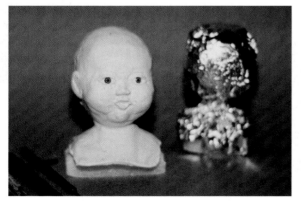

After the facial add-ons have been smoothed, blended, and detailed, add the plastic eyes. Make the lower arms from armatures wrapped with paper clay.

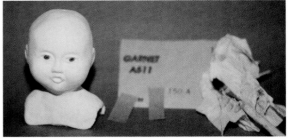

When the clay is completely dry, it's ready for a light sanding with small pieces of fine grade sandpaper. I use the small brush to brush off the sanding dust. Whenever you're sanding, wear rubber gloves and a dust mask. It's a good idea to keep a damp towel on your lap to catch the dust.

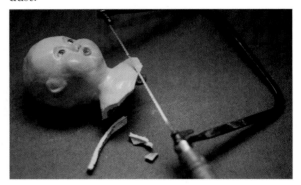

Paint the head and bodice with flesh tone, then paint the lips, eyebrows, cheeks, and any other facial details. The bodice was larger than needed for the doll's body, so I used the saw to trim off the excess and round off the corners. Seal any rough edges with gesso, add some flesh paint, and varnish. I added garlic press hair and painted it yellow.

This photo shows the body with the arms, head, and bodice attached. I pulled a pair of white tights over the cloth legs and right up to arms, put a small hole on each side, and pulled the tights up over the arms so the doll has a one piece body suit.

12"CHILD YURI

MATERIALS

paper clay or papier mâché
2⅜″ x 1⅛″ Styrofoam oval for head armature
5 3″ x 9″ aluminum foil pieces
   (head, arms, legs)
2 taper candles for leg armatures
2 taper candles for arm armatures
black mohair for wig
8″ x 16″ piece of fabric for cloth body
   (pattern for 12″ child body on page 120)
stuffing for cloth body
costume (12″ doll dress pattern on page 133)

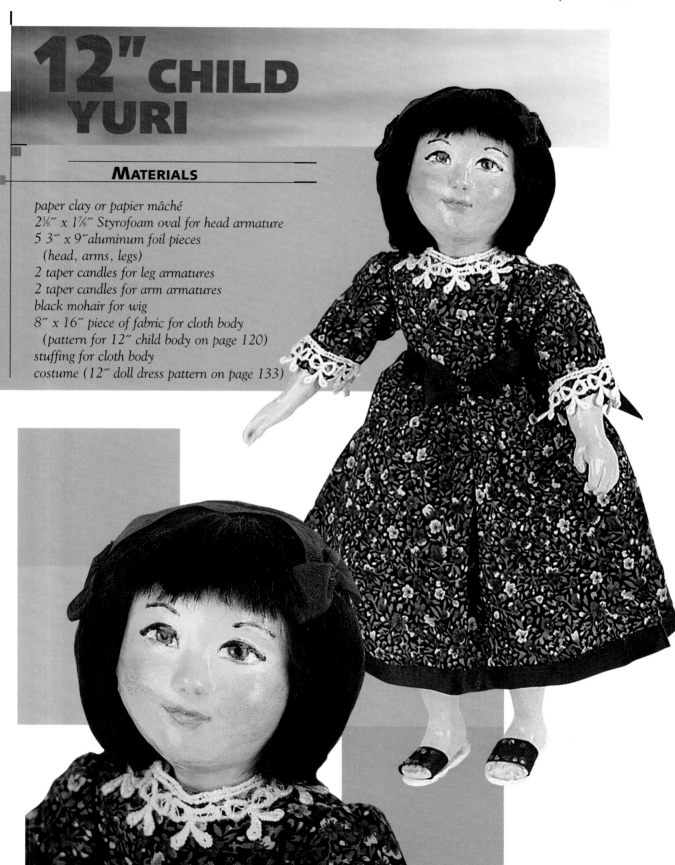

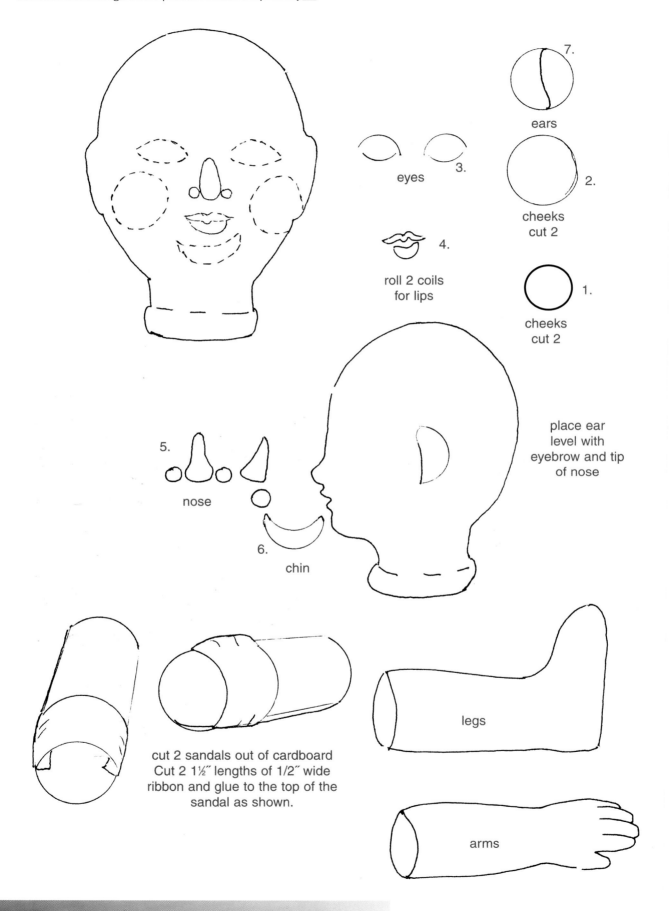

7.

ears

eyes   3.

2.

cheeks
cut 2

4.

roll 2 coils
for lips

1.

cheeks
cut 2

place ear
level with
eyebrow and tip
of nose

5.

nose

6.

chin

cut 2 sandals out of cardboard
Cut 2 1½″ lengths of 1/2″ wide
ribbon and glue to the top of the
sandal as shown.

legs

arms

Make Yuri's lower arm and leg sections from paper clay over armatures as explained in the Techniques section. Draw lines with a needle-point tool to suggest fingers. Repeat for the head/bodice. After you've covered the head armature with 1/4″ thick paper clay, add on features as shown in the diagram. Blend and smooth each piece and add details with a needlepoint tool. Roll coils for the lips and blend them into the face. After the clay has dried, lightly sand and seal with two coats of gesso. When the gesso has dried, apply light flesh to the head/bodice, arms, and legs. I painted on brown eyes and added peach creme rouge to the lips and cheeks. Let dry and brush on a coat of acrylic matte varnish. The head is now ready to have the wig glued on.

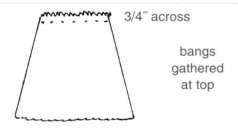

Yuri's hair is made from straight black mohair. Cut a piece 2¼″ x 6″. Fold a piece of wax paper around it and sew the center seam (Yuri's center part). Cut the bangs 2″ long and sew across the top, gathering slightly about 3/4″ across as shown in the illustration.

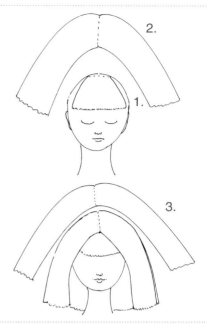

Glue the bangs to the painted head first, then glue on the main hair piece. For a much fuller look, glue on a second layer of mohair over the first. Trim and spray with hair spray and style.

I made this Yuri with a purple chintz body trimmed with lace. She is supported by a doll stand and holds a hula hoop.

KATE & KEISHA

Kate and Keisha in the "Best Friends" sculpture dressed in paper dresses.

MATERIALS

paper clay or papier mâché
2⅜" x 1⅞" Styrofoam oval for head armature
5 3" x 9" pieces aluminum foil
2 taper candles for leg armatures
2 taper candles for arm armatures
light brown small curl mohair for Kate's hair
black mini curls for Keisha
8" x 16" piece of fabric for cloth body (pattern for 12" child body on page 120)
stuffing for cloth body
costume (12" doll dress pattern on page 132)

Kate

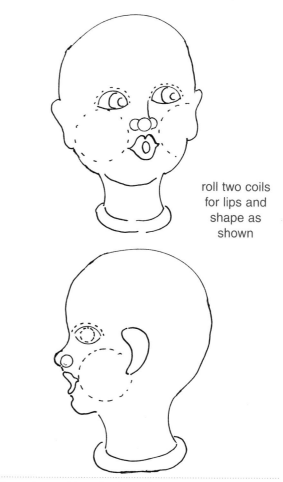

roll two coils for lips and shape as shown

Make Kate using the same instructions, paper clay arms and legs, and cloth body pattern as Yuri, except use the add-ons below to create a different face. Kate has round cheeks, an open mouth, and a dark blond small curl mohair wig. Add the paper clay cutouts and press and smooth them into the head. Keep the paper clay moist so the add-on pieces can be blended and smoothed. You may want to add additional clay so the face and cheeks are nice and round. Use the detail tool, cuticle stick, and round end flat tool to smooth and sculpt each piece.

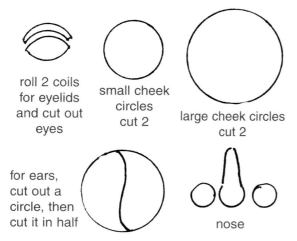

roll 2 coils for eyelids and cut out eyes

small cheek circles cut 2

large cheek circles cut 2

for ears, cut out a circle, then cut it in half

nose

First add the eye cutouts, then the rolled piece for the eyelid. Next add the nose and cheeks (make the cheeks 1/2″ thick and smooth them down around the edges, leaving them high and round in the center). Next add rolled coil lips and the chin and ears (pay special attention to placement of each piece). Roll a coil of paper clay about 1/4″ thick and wrap it around the base of the neck as a "lip" to keep the head in place when it is sewn into the cloth body (this will allow the head to turn from side to side). Let the head dry two days and lightly sand.

Paint with two coats of gesso, then paint the flesh and facial features as desired. I used peach for the lips and cheeks. Mix a dot of peach with a dot of flesh and mix for the cheeks. Outline the eyes with brown and paint the eyebrows. Add some water to the brown and add a few freckles on her nose. Paint the pupil and a circle around the iris black. Let the paint dry and brush on a coat of acrylic matte varnish . The head is now ready to have the wig glued on.

Cut a piece of mohair 2½″ x 7″, place between two pieces of wax paper, and sew a seam down the center. Glue it to the finished doll's head. To curl Kate's hair, start at the top of the head and pick up a few strands of mohair with a needle tool. Spray with hair spray and wrap a strand around the tapered end of a small paint brush handle (for tiny curls, wrap around a large darning needle).

Keisha ▪

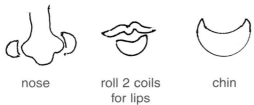

nose   roll 2 coils   chin
for lips

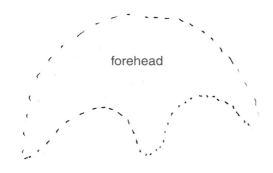

forehead

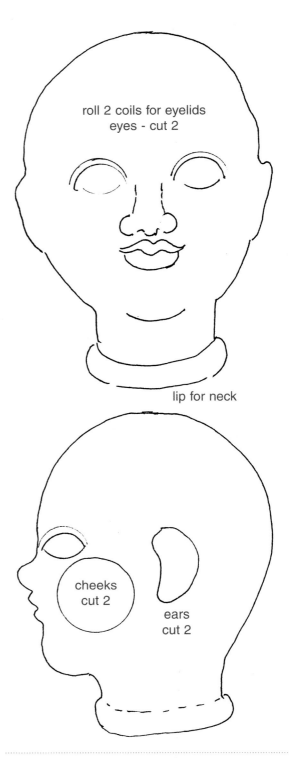

roll 2 coils for eyelids
eyes - cut 2

lip for neck

cheeks
cut 2

ears
cut 2

Keisha is made just like Yuri and Kate, except for her face and hair. Use the diagrams to cut out add-on pieces for Keisha's face from 1/4″ thick paper clay. Add on in this order: nose, cheeks, forehead (blend in with the round end tool and fingers dipped in water), eyes, eyelids (blend in with cuticle stick and detail tool), mouth, chin, ears, and lip around base of neck. Smooth and blend each add-on piece into the paper clay head. Use the round end of a detail tool to poke dimples in both cheeks and chin before the paper clay dries. Let each piece dry, then seal with gesso, let dry, and paint (refer to painting instructions for Cala Vendor).

Keisha has hair made from black mini curls, cut in 2″ and 3″ lengths and glued directly to her head.

This photo shows the technique used to glue on Keisha's hair. Apply glue to the head as shown. Cut out mini curls to the desired length and start at the bottom back of the head. Glue on each piece individually, working upward. The length of hair is short at the bottom and becomes longer as you move upward, so cut the length of the mini curl hair pieces accordingly. I use tacky glue that holds firmly and dries to a clear finish. Use soap and water for clean up.

This mini curl hairstyle is finished. Let dry overnight and gently brush out the next day with a hair prong.

12"
YOUNG PRINCE

MATERIALS

paper clay or papier mâché
2″ Styrofoam ball for head armature
aluminum foil (3″ x 9″)
fabric (8″ x 16″) and stuffing for cloth body
    (12″ child cloth body pattern on page 120)
costume (pattern on page 144)

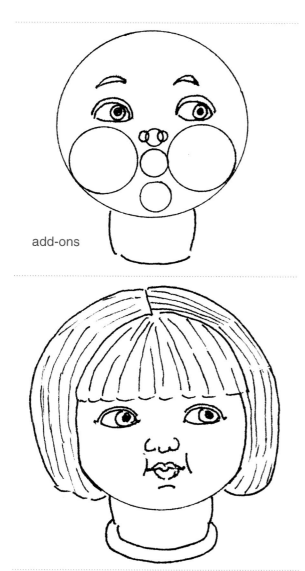

add-ons

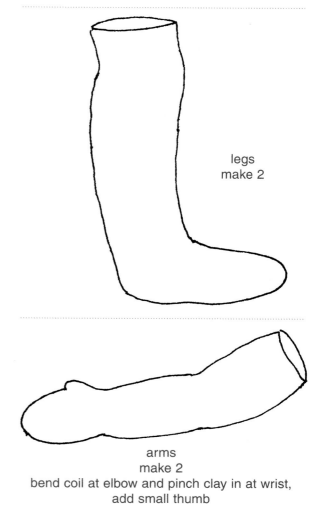

legs
make 2

arms
make 2
bend coil at elbow and pinch clay in at wrist,
add small thumb

The Young Prince is easy to make. Follow the instructions for Yuri, except don't make the arms and legs around armatures, simply roll out coils of paper clay in the palms of your hands and shape them into arm and leg shapes (see the diagram).

Make the head from a 2″ round Styrofoam ball covered in aluminum foil and paper clay as described in the Techniques section. Then add the circle and oval add-ons shown in the diagram. For the eyelids, roll small coils, add them over the eye ovals, and press them in with a detail tool. The lips are two small coils shaped and added over the lip circle. Let all the clay pieces dry.

The hair is easy to cut out and stick to the little round head. It's made from imprinted paper clay (refer to the instructions in the Techniques section). Use the needlepoint tool to cut out and pick up the paper clay hair.

Don't fuss over this figure, just relax and play with the clay. Roll the clay, shape it just a little, and let it dry. After it dries, sand if necessary. Then seal with two coats of gesso and let dry.

Paint flesh tone skin, outline the eyes, paint the whites of the eyes, add brown or blue irises and black pupils. The lips are peach with a light brown line in the center. Rub some peach cream rouge on the cheeks and finish with two coats of satin acrylic varnish. Paint the arms and legs with flesh tone.

Make the cloth body from the same pattern as Yuri. Glue in the arms and legs. Stuff the body, push the head into the neck opening, and sew firmly around the neck.

15"
ALICE

MATERIALS

paper clay or papier mâché
3˝ Styrofoam ball for head armature
aluminum foil
2 taper candles for leg armatures
2 taper candles for arm armatures
9˝ blonde Dynel wig with bangs
fabric (1/4 yard) and stuffing for cloth body
    (15˝ child cloth body pattern on page 121)
costume (15˝ doll dress pattern on
    page 135)

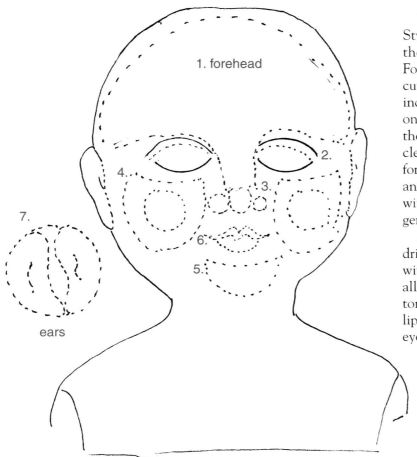

1. forehead

2.

4.

3.

7.

6.

5.

ears

To make this Alice, use a 3″ Styrofoam ball as the basis for the head/bodice armature. Follow the instructions for Yuri, cutting out the add-on pieces as indicated on the diagram. Add on the forehead, two eye circles, the nose circles, the cheek circles, the cheek overlays, the coils for the lips, and the ears. Blend and smooth each add-on piece with a detail tool and your fingers dipped in water.

After the head/bodice has dried, sand if necessary, and seal with two coats of gesso. I painted all the paper clay parts with flesh tone and added blue eyes, peach lips, brown eyelids, and a black eye line.

Make the legs about 3¾″ in circumference and the arms about 3½″ around. Use these drawings to guide you when sculpting the pieces in paper clay. Make the cloth body using the pattern on page 121. I used 1/4 yard peach cotton chintz to make Alice's body, but muslin or felt work well too. Assemble the body according to the directions in the Techniques section.

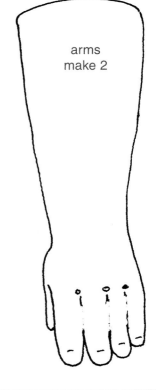

arms
make 2

legs
make 2

17"
MELANIE & SCARLETT

MATERIALS

paper clay or papier mâché
2½" x 1⅛" Styrofoam ovals for head armatures
aluminum foil (3" x 9", 3" x 12")
2 taper candles for leg armatures
2 taper candles for arm armatures
mohair for Scarlett's wig
fabric and stuffing for cloth bodies
    (17" cloth body pattern
    on page 122)
costume (17" doll
    dress pattern on
    page 137)

Follow the basic instructions to make the dolls using paper clay and the pattern for the 17" cloth body. I recommend using paper clay for these dolls because it has a beautiful smooth porcelain look when completed. A one pound package of the paper clay will be enough for both dolls. Make the heads, arms, and legs from paper clay.

Melanie |■

Melanie's
head & hair

add-on cutouts

imprinted
paper clay hair

bun

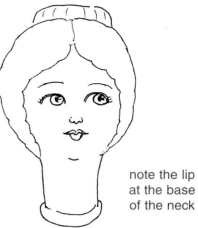

note the lip
at the base
of the neck

Melanie is the easier of the two, so make her first. She has a much simpler modeling style than Scarlett and a much simpler hairstyle.

Make the oval head with just a neck, no bodice. The head retains much of the egg shape with very simple modeling of features (tiny nose/coils over eyes and very small coil lips). The face and neck are covered with 1/4″ paper clay. Add a small piece of clay for the nose as shown and blend it into the face by gently pushing in with your thumbs and a detail tool. Make two small circles and add them to either side for nostrils. The eye sockets can be suggested by gently pushing in on each side of the nose with your thumb and index finger. Add a little bit of paper clay at the chin line so the chin doesn't recede and add small coils for the lips. Use the cuticle and detail tools to add detail around the lips, nose, and eyes.

After all the features are placed and blended, let the

head dry for two days, then inspect it closely. You may want to add more paper clay to the dry piece to fill in spots and to round out the features. Just add the piece, push it in place with your fingers, and smooth it with a detail tool. Let dry completely, sand and seal with two coats of gesso. When the gesso is dry, the head is ready to be painted.

Paint two coats of flesh tone acrylic paint on the head and neck. Pencil in the facial features and use a small pointed detail brush to paint the whites of the eyes. Let dry. Outline the eye with a fine black outline. Paint blue eyes, black pupils, and black eyebrows. Paint the lips pink or peach with a darker pink as a shadow line separating the lips. Rub in creme peach rouge for the cheeks. When the paint is dry, brush on a light coat of acrylic matte varnish. Let dry. Apply a second coat of varnish.

Melanie's hair is imprinted paper clay with a bun on top. Cut out the pieces of clay and imprint lines with a crochet thread card. Cut one section to fit the right side and wrap it around to the back. Repeat for the left side. Form a small circle for the bun on top of her head, about 1/2″ thick. Place it on top of her head and push it into the imprinted clay hair. When the clay has dried, seal with two coats of gesso, paint, and varnish.

To make the arms for both dolls, wrap aluminum foil (3″ x 10″) around taper candles and start at the elbow to cover the armature completely with 1/2″ thick paper clay. Using your fingers and the round end of a sculpting tool, smooth and shape the arm. This is the basic sculpting method for the shovel hand. Add a small thumb. Let dry, seal with gesso, and paint.

Make the legs for both dolls. Cover the armatures completely with paper clay. The aluminum foil is bent up to form the foot. The diagram below shows the right size. Let dry, seal with gesso, and paint. Paint two thin coats of flesh tone acrylic paint on the arms and legs. Let the first coat dry completely before applying the next. Shoes can be painted on the feet. When the paint is dry, apply two coats of acrylic matte varnish.

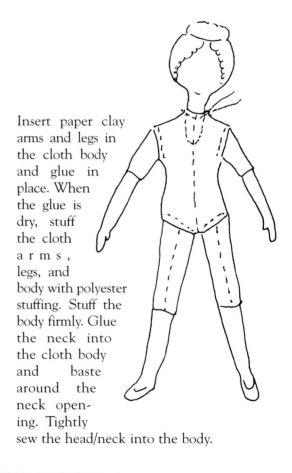

Insert paper clay arms and legs in the cloth body and glue in place. When the glue is dry, stuff the cloth arms, legs, and body with polyester stuffing. Stuff the body firmly. Glue the neck into the cloth body and baste around the neck opening. Tightly sew the head/neck into the body.

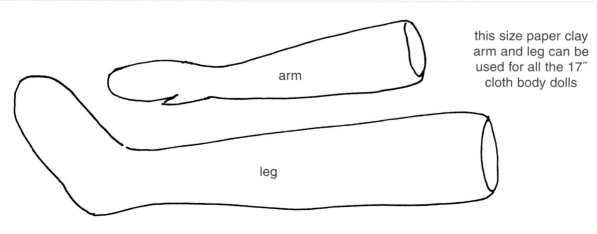

arm

leg

this size paper clay arm and leg can be used for all the 17″ cloth body dolls

Scarlett ▪

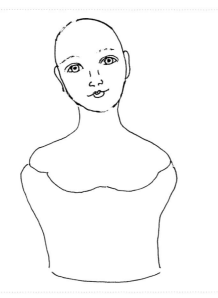

Make Scarlett with a bodice and a slightly turned head. When shaping the neck and bodice, gently tilt the aluminum foil and turn just about 1/2″ to the left.

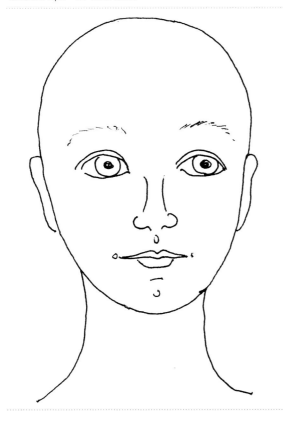

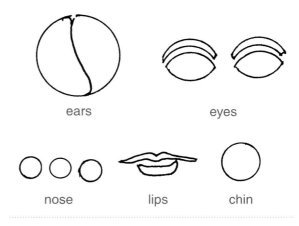

ears   eyes

nose   lips   chin

Push the paper clay in with a cuticle stick around the eyes to make an oval eye shape. Push in for the indentation of the eyelid and add a coil of paper clay rolled about 1/8″ round. Add on the nose pieces and blend in. Use the point of a toothpick to make her nostrils flare. Add more paper clay coils for the lips and blend. Use a detail tool to smooth the clay upward to form the upper lip and downward for the bottom lip. Use the round end of a detail tool to push in dimples under the nose, on either side of the lips, and in the chin. To make the ears, cut small half circles of paper clay and place them on either side of the head as shown.

After all the features are placed and blended, set the head aside and let dry for two days. When the head is dry, look it over closely. You may need to add more paper clay to the dry piece to fill in spots and to round out the features. Just add the piece, push it in place with your fingers, and smooth it with a detail tool. Let dry completely, sand and seal with two coats of gesso. When the gesso is dry, the head is ready to be painted. Refer to the painting instructions for Melanie. I chose green eyes for Scarlett.

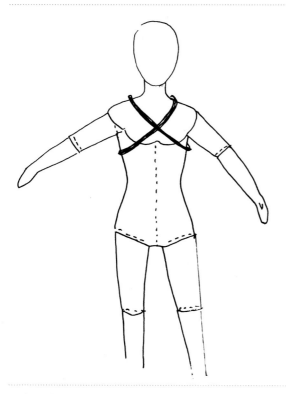

secure with rubber bands

Glue the arms and legs to the cloth body. Glue the bodice and place it over the top of the cloth body. Hold it in place with rubber bands until the glue dries.

The wig will be the very last item to make and add to the doll. I used auburn small curl mohair to make Scarlett's wig. Cut a piece of mohair 3˝ x 14˝. Thread your sewing machine to match the mohair. Place the mohair between two pieces of wax paper and sew a center part down the middle. Glue the mohair piece to the head. Secure with rubber bands until the glue dries.

Scarlett's hair is styled with long flowing curls cascading down her back. The mohair is already curled with small waves throughout. Gently pull a small piece of hair up on either side, using a large needle to separate the hair and tie with a ribbon to match the color of her dress. The rest of the hair will be styled with full curls and a few small curls around her face. Lightly spray each piece of mohair and wrap each large curl around the handle of a small paint brush and gently pull it off. Repeat for all the large curls. Use a large needle to make the smaller curls around her face. Cover the curls with a hair net until dry. (The same technique is used to make Beauty's mohair wig.)

17" ENGLISH DOLL

MATERIALS

paper clay or papier mâché
2½" x 1⅛" Styrofoam oval for head armature
aluminum foil (3" x 9")
2 taper candles for leg armatures
2 taper candles for arm armatures
fabric and stuffing for cloth body (17" cloth
*   body pattern on page 122)*
costume

Make the cloth body for a 17" doll. Follow the basic instructions for sculpting a doll head over an armature. There's not much sculpting to the head, just add a little nose and chin. The eyes are hand-painted. The shovel hands are the same as for Melanie, as are the legs and feet. This doll has small feet with painted on slippers. The hair is papier mâché with a crochet chain stitch braid around her head. Hair of that period (1100) was worn in long braids or wrapped around the head and covered by the head drapery, called a wimple. Use the drawing for Melanie for facial add-ons and follow the instructions for the paper clay hair add-on.

This is an easy project with very little modeling needed for great results. You can even paint on features without any paper clay add-ons (use the Melanie drawing for guidance).

This doll was made in the early 1970s and the papier mâché head is as smooth as the day I completed her.

17" CHINA DOLL

MATERIALS

paper clay or papier mâché
2½″ x 1⅞″ Styrofoam oval for head armature
aluminum foil (3″ x 11″)
2 taper candles for leg armatures
2 taper candles for arm armatures
fabric (1/4 yard) and stuffing for cloth
   body (17″ cloth body pattern on
   page 122)
costume (China Doll dress pattern
   on page 140)

The China Doll is another variation of the basic Melanie doll. Make the cloth body for a 17″ doll. Follow the basic instructions for sculpting a doll head over an armature. The arms and legs are paper clay, made like Melanie's. The only real difference is in the hair. Cover the head with imprinted paper clay hair. Make three braids of strips of paper clay and push them into the head as shown. When the clay dries, paint the hair black, and varnish.

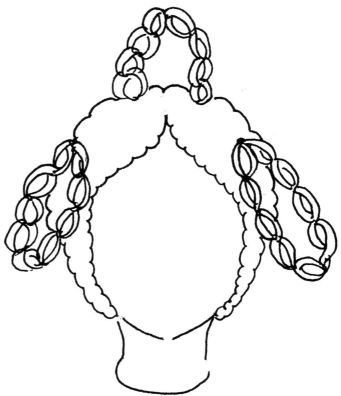

China doll has a very tiny nose and chin added, but the face is an easy one to sculpt. Very little sculpting is needed. If you want to add more sculpting detail, use the add-ons for Melanie.

17" QUEEN ELIZABETH I

MATERIALS

paper clay or papier mâché

2⅜" x 1⅞" Styrofoam oval for head armature

aluminum foil

fabric (1/4 yard) and stuffing for cloth body
  (17" cloth body pattern on page 122)

costume

This doll's hair is made with 1/2″ thick clay imprinted with a lace pattern. Cut out two heart shaped pieces of clay, one for the back of the head and one for the front. Cut the front heart into two pieces, one for each side of the face. Build up in the front to form the heart shaped hairdo. Shape and press the clay hair to the clay head. Let dry, seal with gesso, and paint as usual. After the hair has been painted and varnished, glue on pearls and additional trimmings.

In this queen's time, an abundance of lace, beads, and braiding were used to decorate the rich gowns. Necklaces, rings, and earrings were set with semi-precious stones. She wears a green velvet gown with two yards of 1½″ white cotton lace gathered to fit around her neck as a ruff. All of these decorations can be added to Queen Elizabeth's gown and hairdo. The hair styles were frizzed and curled and Elizabeth wore her red hair like a heart at the crown and braided in the back. She has small curls all around her high forehead.

Make the cloth body for a 17″ doll. Follow the basic instructions for sculpting a doll head over an armature. There's not much sculpting to the head, just add a little nose and chin. The eyes are hand-painted. This particular doll has cloth arms and legs, but you can make paper clay arms and legs over armatures if you prefer.

I used antique flesh for her skin tone and red, orange, and burnt umber mixed for her hair. If you can't find antique flesh acrylic paint, mix a little white in the flesh acrylic paint. I painted her shoes red. This is a beautiful doll to add to your collection or to give as a gift.

front

BEAUTY & THE BEAST

17" Beauty ▪

MATERIALS

paper clay or papier mâché
2½″ x 1⅞″ Styrofoam oval for head
*   armature*
aluminum foil (3″ x 11″)
2 taper candles for leg armatures
2 taper candles for arm armatures
dark blond small curl mohair for
*   wig*
fabric (1/4 yard) and stuffing for
*   cloth body (17″ cloth body*
*   pattern on page 122)*
costume (17″ doll dress pattern
*   on page 137)*

Make the cloth body for a 17″ doll. Follow the basic instructions for sculpting a doll head over an armature and use the same add-on pieces as Scarlett. Beauty has a turned head armature with a bodice similar to Scarlett. As you see in the photo, lace and pearls have been added to the mohair wig. The eyes are hand-painted.

The wig is made of dark blonde small curl mohair with a center part. It is styled with each side pulled up and tied in the back with curls down the back, similar to Scarlett's. Extra curls can be made and glued to the back. The costume is made of pink silk with a beige silk print petticoat.

20" Prince/22" Beast

MATERIALS

paper clay or papier mâché
3 1/16" x 2" Styrofoam oval for Prince head armature
6" Styrofoam egg for Beast head armature
aluminum foil (4" x 12", 6" x 12" for arms and legs)
20" flexible plastic armature for body
2 taper candles for Prince leg armatures
2 taper candles for Prince arm armatures
dark brown small curl mohair for Prince's wig and beard
fabric (1/2 yard) and stuffing for cloth body (use 20" Old Chris cloth body pattern on page 132)
fake fur fabric for Beast's head, hands, feet
1/2 yard brown felt for Beast costume
Prince costume (pattern on page146)
small pieces of silk

This is two dolls in one. The Prince is under the tattered cloak and rough head of the Beast. First make the 20" Prince. The Beast is really just a costume over the Prince.

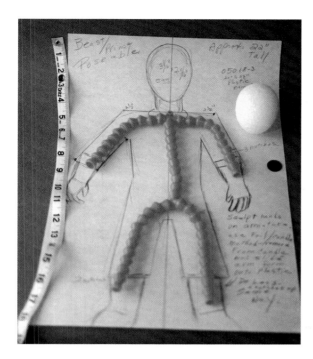

Begin by making the cloth body for the 20″ Old Chris figure. Cut out the pattern from unbleached muslin. Sew up the seams, leaving openings inside the legs.

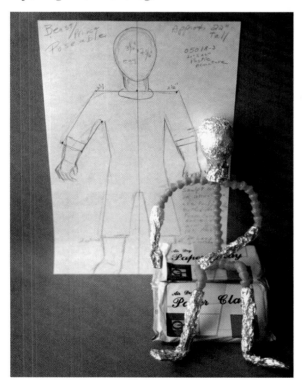

Cover the Styrofoam oval with aluminum foil as shown and place it on the plastic armature. Add aluminum foil to the plastic armature to shape the lower arms and legs. This is just to get

an idea of how long the appendages will be. Remove the foil pieces from the plastic armature.

Cut cotton batting into 1″ strips and wrap it around the flexible plastic armature. Tie the batting on with thread. Slide the muslin body over the armature and slide the arms into the cloth. Pull the cloth down over the plastic legs and add additional stuffing in front and back, up through the shoulders. Sew up the seam on the inside of the legs from left to right, folding 1/4″ of fabric inside. Set the body aside and sculpt the head, arms, and legs from paper clay.

Sculpt the Prince's head/neck, lower arms, and lower legs over armatures. Follow the basic sculpting directions in the Techniques section. Add ears and other facial features with extra paper clay pieces blended into the head. Let the clay dry completely, then sand lightly and seal with two coats of gesso. Use the photo as a sculpting and painting guide. When the paint is dry, apply two coats of varnish and glue on mohair hair, mustache, and goatee if desired.

To make the hollow beast head that will fit over the Prince's head, wrap a 6″ Styrofoam egg with aluminum foil, folding, pressing, and shaping the foil over the egg to make a dome (4″ top to bottom) open at the base. Tape a 2″ length of a 1¼″ cardboard tube on the front of the dome for the snout. Do not remove the Styrofoam egg until the papier mâché sculpture has been formed over the armature and the mâché has dried. After the mâché on the head has dried completely, slide it off the egg so the head is hollow.

This photo shows the finished head piece and the armature, both supported by empty detergent bottles.

On this sculpture I used gray instant papier mâché so it looks different than the white paper

clay used on others. Mix the papier mâché as directed on the package and roll it out to 1/2″ thick.

Cut out strips to cover the foil head, smoothing it with the round end of a sculpting tool and your fingers. Start at the back and work to the top of the head, around the sides, and then to the front. Dip your fingers in water occasionally. Wrap mâché around the nose and smooth it with your fingers. Add large rolled coils for the eyelids and horns. Add pointed ears and ovals for eyes. Add extra pieces of mâché to build up the forehead, nose, eyes, and lips. Blend the add-ons into the face and set aside to dry.

Cut out the hands and feet from papier mâché rolled 1/2″ thick. Reverse the patterns after cutting out one, so you'll have one right and one left of each. Cut out ten fingernails and ten toenails.

Here the head is completely dried with cardboard teeth added. Prop the hands and feet over wooden dowels so they'll dry with a slight curve in the fingers and toes. After the hands have dried completely, glue the mâché nails on the ends of the fingers.

After the papier mâché has dried (usually two days), sand slightly, but not too smooth. The Beast should be roughly textured. Seal all the pieces with four coats of gesso. Apply two coats of brown acrylic paint. Let dry. Apply a thin coat of black paint and wipe off, leaving only shadows in the texture. Paint on the features. Let dry and varnish all the pieces. Apply gesso and varnish inside the hollow head too. Glue on the fake fur at the wrists and ankles. Glue brown mohair on the head as hair and on the face as a beard.

patterns for Beast's hands and feet

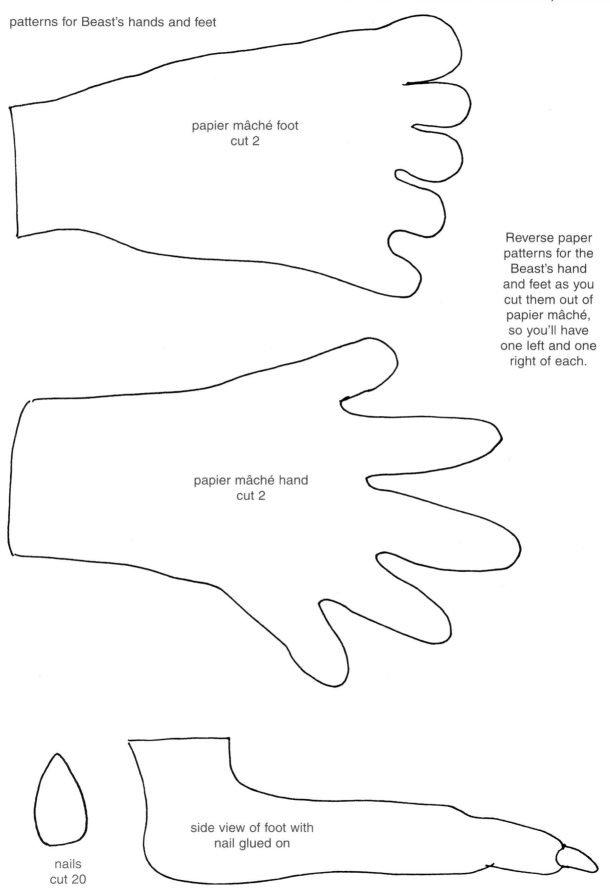

papier mâché foot
cut 2

Reverse paper patterns for the Beast's hand and feet as you cut them out of papier mâché, so you'll have one left and one right of each.

papier mâché hand
cut 2

nails
cut 20

side view of foot with
nail glued on

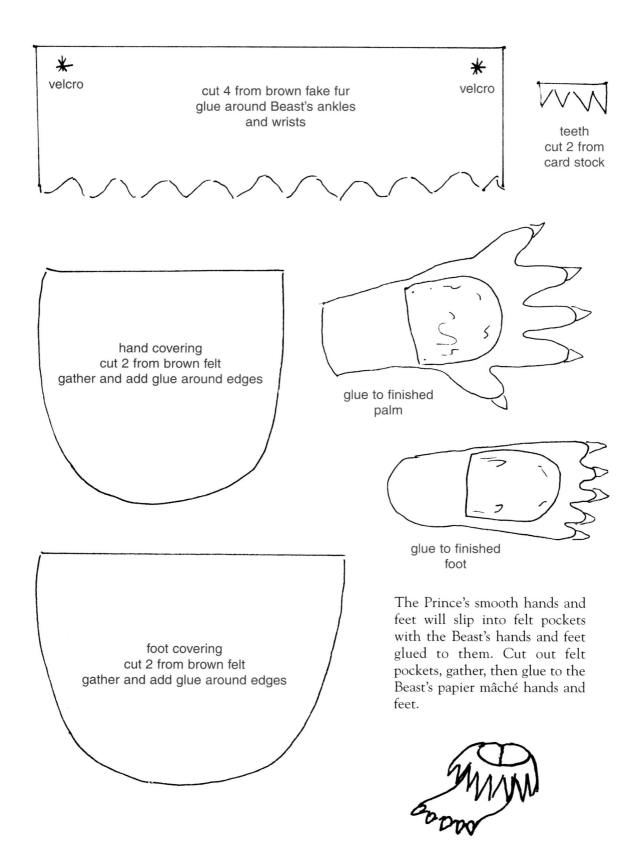

velcro

cut 4 from brown fake fur
glue around Beast's ankles
and wrists

velcro

teeth
cut 2 from
card stock

hand covering
cut 2 from brown felt
gather and add glue around edges

glue to finished
palm

glue to finished
foot

foot covering
cut 2 from brown felt
gather and add glue around edges

The Prince's smooth hands and feet will slip into felt pockets with the Beast's hands and feet glued to them. Cut out felt pockets, gather, then glue to the Beast's papier mâché hands and feet.

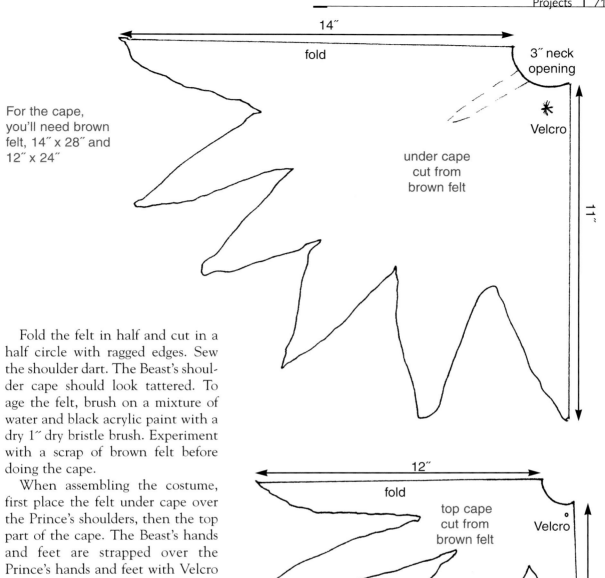

14″

fold

3″ neck opening

Velcro

under cape cut from brown felt

11″

For the cape, you'll need brown felt, 14″ x 28″ and 12″ x 24″

12″

fold

top cape cut from brown felt

Velcro

5″

Fold the felt in half and cut in a half circle with ragged edges. Sew the shoulder dart. The Beast's shoulder cape should look tattered. To age the felt, brush on a mixture of water and black acrylic paint with a dry 1″ dry bristle brush. Experiment with a scrap of brown felt before doing the cape.

When assembling the costume, first place the felt under cape over the Prince's shoulders, then the top part of the cape. The Beast's hands and feet are strapped over the Prince's hands and feet with Velcro tabs on the fake fur that has been glued on the Beast's hands and feet. The broad brimmed hat is put in the right hand and the rose in the left hand of the Beast.

15" TASHA

MATERIALS

paper clay or papier mâché
2½" x 1⅞" Styrofoam oval for head armature
aluminum foil (3" x 10")
gray mohair for wig
fabric and stuffing for cloth body (use 17"
   cloth body pattern on page 122)
costume (use 17" doll dress pattern on
   page 137)

Tasha is a beautiful little old lady with a gray mohair wig, sculpted paper clay high-top shoes, and little hands with tiny fingers.

Make the cloth body first. Since Tasha is 15″, you'll need to reduce the pattern for a 17″ doll by 5/8″ all around. Shorten the arm and leg patterns by one inch.

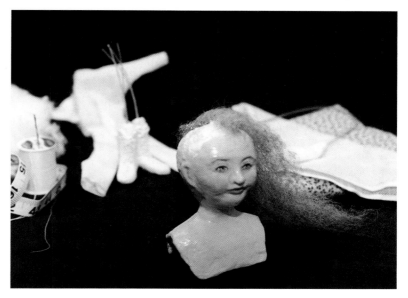

To sculpt Tasha's face, make the head with bodice armature, following the instructions for Melanie and using the same add-ons. Add wrinkles in the paper clay around her eyes, forehead, and mouth with the detail tool. Use the round end to suggest a very light line in her forehead. After the head has dried, sand if necessary, and seal with two coats of gesso. Paint with flesh paint, then add blue eyes and peach rouge on the cheeks. When the paint has dried, apply two coats of varnish.

Tasha's arms and legs are simply rolled coils of paper clay shaped and formed to look like arms and legs (refer to the diagrams on page 74). Bend the end of the legs to form a foot.

For the arms, squeeze in slightly at the wrist, flatten the hands, and make fingers with a needle tool pressed into the clay to make lines (refer to the diagrams on page 74). Separate the fingers and gently shape them using a small detail brush. The fingers are so small it's easy to shape them with the tiny bristles dipped in water and wiped on a paper towel.

Roll out paper clay to 1/2″ thick and cut out the boots using the pattern on page 74. Roll two coils 1/8″ and use as shoelaces crisscrossed up the front of the boot to resemble shoelaces and a bow. Seal the paper clay pieces with gesso

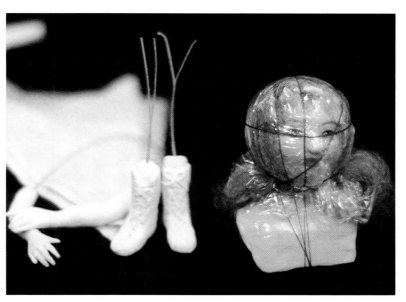

and paint as desired. Apply two coats of varnish.

After you've finished the head/bodice, cut a 2½″ x 10″ piece of gray mohair. Brush glue on top of the doll's head and place the mohair on the top with the part centered.

Wrap with plastic wrap and tie with thread down the center and around the head to hold hair in place until the glue dries. Assemble the cloth body and paper clay arms, legs, and head.

Use these diagrams as a guide for Tasha

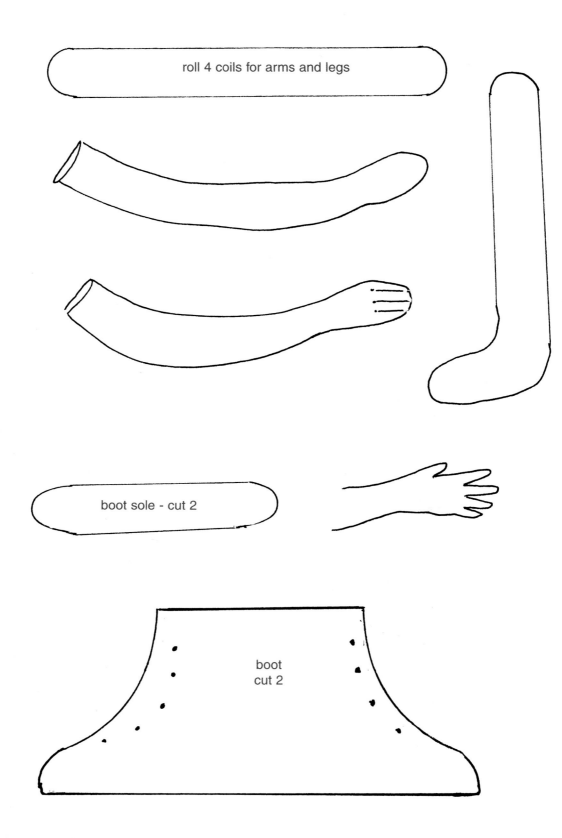

roll 4 coils for arms and legs

boot sole - cut 2

boot
cut 2

22" ADELAIDE

MATERIALS

paper clay or papier mâché
3½" x 2⁵/₁₆" Styrofoam oval for head armature
aluminum foil (6" x 12")
2 taper candles for leg armatures
2 taper candles for arm armatures
fabric and stuffing for cloth body (20"-22"
    cloth body pattern on page 124)
costume (22" doll dress pattern on page 142)
Note: I used 2/3 yard cotton or silk and 2
yards of 1/4"-wide ribbon for the dress and
1/2 yard bastiste for the slip and lace.

Adelaide is a molded hair papier mâché doll in the style of the 1830s, with a slim waist, full skirt, puff sleeves, and bows.

Make the head/bodice armature according the directions in the Techniques section. Use a piece of aluminum foil 6″ x 12″. Make arm and leg armatures over taper candles as described in the Techniques section, using 5″ x 10″ pieces of aluminum foil. The head/bodice, hair, arms, and legs are all made of paper clay.

Cut out the add-ons for the face and bust. Cut all add-ons from 1/4″ thick paper clay except the add-ons for the cheeks and bust which should be thicker in the center and 1/4″ at the edges. Apply them to the head/bodice, blend and smooth.

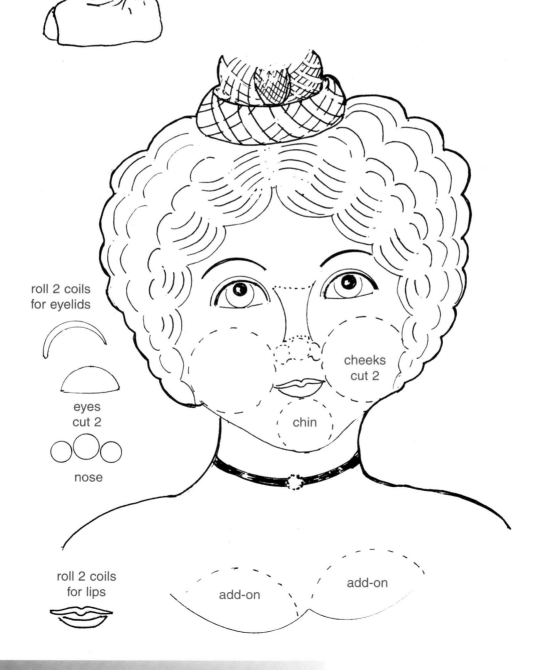

roll 2 coils
for eyelids

eyes
cut 2

nose

roll 2 coils
for lips

cheeks
cut 2

chin

add-on

add-on

The finished head shown was made with papier mâché. The one in progress is being made with paper clay. Circles of clay have been added for the cheeks, chin, bodice and an extra piece on the shoulders to round them off. The pieces have been added for the nose and smoothed in. Use your fingers to form and shape the clay by wetting and pushing the clay. Keep water and paper towels handy.

Adding on, smoothing in, and adding detail to the face. Check your work from all sides. Turn the head upside down and look at the eyes, nose, and mouth. Look at it from the side, place it in front of the mirror and look at its reflection. Errors are easy to spot and can be easily corrected with paper clay. If you are not finished with the sculpting at the end of the day, place the head in a sealed plastic bag to keep it moist.

The entire head has been covered, the features built up, and the clay added to the bodice. Dip the sculpting tools in water as you use them and smooth the mâché. Use the orange stick to define the details around the eyes and mouth, pressing and pushing on the mâché gently to shape the eye. Press in on the outer and inner corners of the eye. Push up a line of mâché for the eyelid on both eyes. Add more mâché as needed. Roll a small coil and place it over each eye and blend in with an orange stick.

To make the hair: Roll out the paper clay to 1/2″ thick. Cut out the hair patterns on page 79 with a needlepoint tool. Place the pieces on the head and gently press. Use the round edge sculpting tool to press ridges into the hair and a comb to press in lines to resemble hair. Roll small circles for curls and press them to the head. Press the comb into each curl to give it the look of hair. This was a time-consuming process but well worth it. The photo of the three Adelaides shows three different hairstyles and faces and three dresses, two of cotton and one of silk.

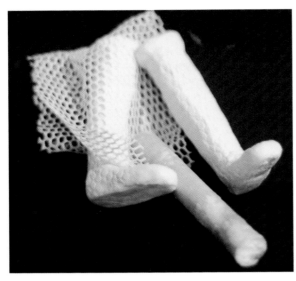

While the paper clay legs are still moist, press a mesh pattern into the clay. Roll it into the clay with a round piece of wood. This will create the look of mesh stockings. Paint white.

This photo shows an assembled body where the head/bodice, arms, and legs have been attached to the cloth body. Also shown are the paper clay pieces after the gesso has been applied, but before they've been painted.

Using a 1/2″ wide flat glaze brush, apply two coats of flesh colored paint. Let dry between coats. Paint the hair with two coats of black acrylic, eyes with blue, and lips with a mix of white, mauve, and red. Paint in the features as shown in the photos. I used pink creme rouge rubbed into the cheek area and blended with a cotton swab. Dab some on the tip of the nose and on the chin and blend. When all is dry, apply two coats of satin acrylic varnish.

The shoes can be painted right on the paper clay feet. When you are finished with all the painting and the paint has dried, brush on a thin coat of acrylic varnish. Brush on at least two smooth coats of varnish. Dry thoroughly.

Make the cloth body using the pattern for a 22″ doll. I chose unbleached muslin for the body because it is easy to work with and is readily available. Measure the paper clay arms and legs and adjust the size of the arm opening of the pattern to fit. Sew the darts in the back and front. Start on the left side of the body and sew from the leg, up the side, under the arm. Sew up the right side. Leave openings for the arms and legs. Leave an opening at the neck for turning the body and stuffing. Turn the body and add lace or hem the openings.

Apply glue around the tops of the paper clay arms and legs. Insert them in the cloth body, adding glue to the arm and leg openings. After the glue has dried and the arms and legs are firmly in place, stuff the body using small pieces of cotton or polyester stuffing. Push each piece into the legs first, then into the waist, arms, and bodice. Stuff firmly. Sew up the seam at the neck and apply glue to the underside of the paper clay bodice. Press the bodice over the cloth body and secure with rubber bands until the glue is dry. I place the rubber bands over each shoulder and down to the center of the legs. This holds the bodice nice and tight until the glue is dry, usually overnight.

Adelaide hair patterns

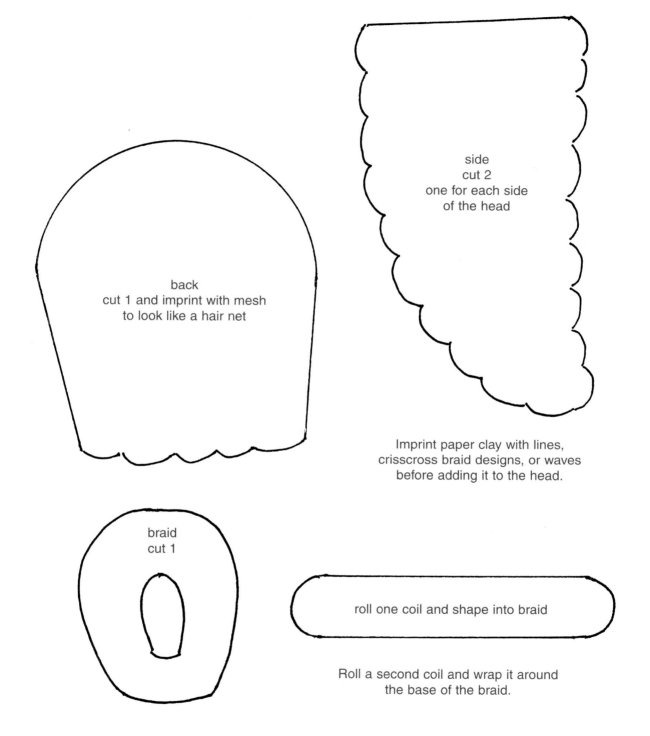

back
cut 1 and imprint with mesh
to look like a hair net

side
cut 2
one for each side
of the head

Imprint paper clay with lines,
crisscross braid designs, or waves
before adding it to the head.

braid
cut 1

roll one coil and shape into braid

Roll a second coil and wrap it around
the base of the braid.

20" CALA VENDOR

MATERIALS

paper clay or papier mâché
2⁵⁄₁₆″ x 3¹⁄₁₆″ Styrofoam oval for head
 armature
aluminum foil (3 pieces 4″ x 12″)
2 taper candles for leg armatures
2 taper candles for arm armatures
black mini curl .50 oz. polypropylene
 filament hair
18mm porcelain teeth
fabric and stuffing for cloth body
 (20″-22″ cloth body pattern on
 page 124)
costume (22″ doll dress pattern
 on page 142)

I found a drawing of the Cala Vendor in a book on the history of New Orleans. In 1886, Cala Vendor was out early in the morning selling rice fritters from her covered bowl. The cry of the vendor was, "Bels calas, touts chauds (Fine fritters, very hot)." When I designed and made my doll, I named her after the rice fritters she sold.

Make the head/bodice with paper clay over the foil-covered Styrofoam oval as instructed in the Techniques section. Cut out the add-ons from paper clay rolled 1/4˝ thick. Start with the forehead piece and add ovals for the eyes and coils for the eyelids. Cut the three circles for the nose, two for the cheeks, and one small circle for the chin. For the ears, cut one circle and

cut it in half. Add two half circles to shape the bodice. Blend them into the head with sculpting tools and fingers dipped in water. Cut one oval for the mouth. After the face has been sculpted but before the paper clay dries, open the lips with an orange stick and press in the porcelain teeth to make the indentations for them. Remove the teeth and let the paper clay dry. Sand if necessary and seal with two coats of gesso.

Paint the head/bodice with 2 oz. dark flesh mixed with 2 oz. dark brown. Apply two coats and let dry. Paint on one coat of dark flesh mixed with varnish and a drop of black paint. Brush on around the eyes, nose, and mouth. Gently wipe it off with lint free cheesecloth. Let dry. Rouge the cheeks and lips with bronze rouge. Highlight the nose, cheeks, and chin with dark flesh mixed with varnish. Paint the lips with a mix of dark flesh and a drop of red paint. Let dry. Use copper colored cream rouge on the cheeks and lips (I used one of my own makeup rouge sticks). Blend in the rouge with a flat glaze brush.

Carefully apply a coat of satin varnish. Let dry and apply another coat of copper rouge. Wipe with cotton and then apply the last coat of satin varnish.

After the head is completely finished, put the porcelain teeth back in the mouth with super-tacky glue.

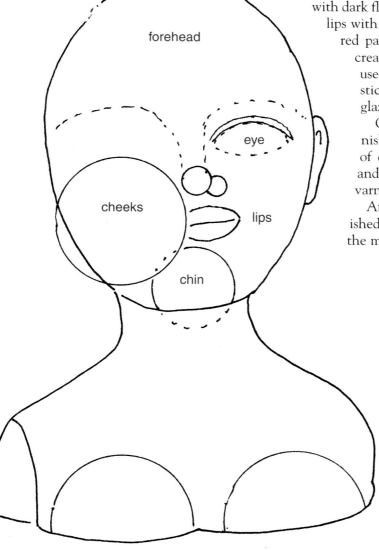

forehead

eye

cheeks

lips

chin

Add two 1/2 circles to shape the bodice.

Cala's hair is made from black mini curl poly-propylene filament. Each mini curl has been cut and glued directly to her head. Cut out curls, 1″, 2″, and 3″ long. Glue on curls one at a time, starting at base of the scalp with the shortest curls and moving up the back and then to the sides of the head with the longer curls. You can tie five strands of curls together and glue it on instead of individually if you prefer.

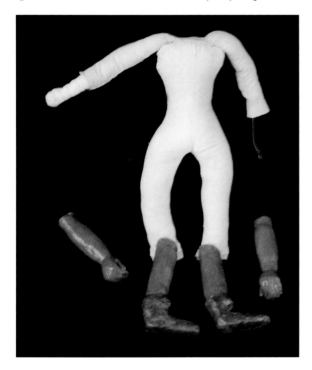

Make the paper clay arms and legs as directed in the Techniques chapter. Wrap a 7½″ x 9″

piece of aluminum foil around each candle. Cover with paper clay, let dry, seal with gesso, and paint with the same colors you used on the head/bodice. Roll out clay cutouts and wrap them around the leg to create boots. Use a pencil point to press in holes for shoe laces which are made with paper clay coils. When the clay has dried, seal with gesso and paint brown.

Make the cloth body from the pattern for a 20″-22″ figure. The photo shows the body ready for assembly. The cloth arms have been hand-stitched across the bodice and a wire has been inserted through the arms. The lower arm on the left has been wrapped with cotton, while the one on the right shows the bare wire. Before attaching the paper clay arms, wrap the wire on the right with cotton too. Apply glue inside and around the top 1/2″ of the paper clay pieces. Slide the paper clay arms over the wire and pull the cloth over them. Tie with thread until the glue dries. Insert the legs into the cloth openings and pull the cloth down over the paper clay leg. Tie thread around the cloth until the glue dries then remove the thread.

This photo shows the completed doll before costuming. The costumed Cala Vendor is mounted on a wood base with a wood dowel inserted in the back of the body. She carries a basket made of paper clay with wood shavings embedded in the clay.

Cala patterns

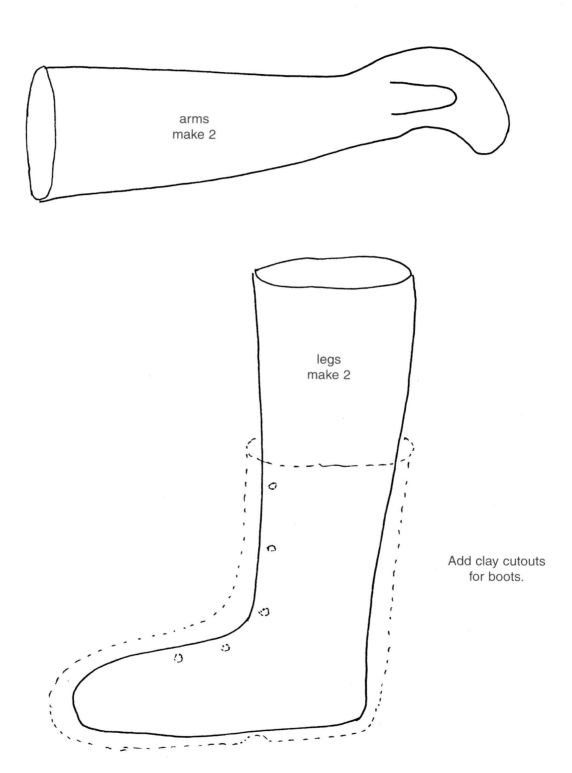

arms
make 2

legs
make 2

Add clay cutouts
for boots.

20" HARLEQUIN

MATERIALS

paper clay or papier mâché
2½″ Styrofoam ball for head armature
aluminum foil (4″ x 8″ for head, 5″ x 8″ for
    arms and legs)
2 taper candles for leg armatures
2 taper candles for arm armatures
fabric and stuffing for cloth body (20″-22″
    cloth body pattern on page 124)
costume

Harlequin was made as a self portrait. I made the Harlequin costume for a New Orleans masquerade party and made a replica for this doll using leftover scraps of fabric and sequins.

Make the head/bodice with paper clay over the foil-covered Styrofoam ball as instructed in the Techniques section. Cut out the add-ons from paper clay rolled 1/4″ thick. Cut one forehead, two eyes, and roll two coils for eyelids and two more for below the eyes. Cut out the circles for the nose, cheeks, and chin. Cut two ears. Roll small coils for the lips and one larger coil from 1/2″ thick paper clay for the base of the neck. Blend all the add-ons into the head with sculpting tools and fingers dipped in water. Start with the forehead piece, nose, eyes, and cheeks, blending each addition until smooth. Add the coils for the lips and eyes and smooth the clay. Add a coil of clay around the neck to later help secure the head/bodice to the cloth body.

Look over your work carefully. Make any additions or subtractions of clay. The paper clay head should measure 8¼″ in circumference. When you're satisfied, set the head aside to dry, then sand it carefully. Seal with two coats of gesso.

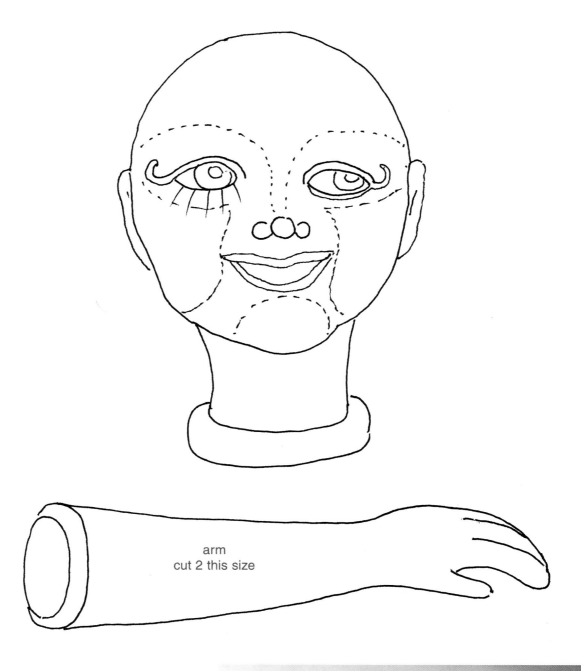

arm
cut 2 this size

Paint the head with two coats of white paint. Paint the lips red and outline the eyes in black. I didn't add any hair on this doll.

Make the arms and legs of paper clay over armatures as explained in the Techniques section. The arms and legs both measure 5½″ long. Add a coil around the top of the arm and leg sections to help hold the cloth body on. After you've sanded and sealed with gesso, paint white.

Here's the completed body before costuming. The bald head is painted white. Harlequin is made into a sculpture by gluing a 7/16″ wood dowel 16″ long into a wood base 6″ x 8″ x 1″ and mounting the completed figure by sliding the dowel into the back of the cloth body up into the neck of the figure. I painted the base of the stand with colors from the costume.

20" JINGLES

MATERIALS

paper clay or papier mâché
3″ Styrofoam ball for head armature
aluminum foil
mohair for hair
fabric and stuffing for felt body (Jingles cloth
   body pattern on page 126)
costume (Jingles costume pattern on page
   149)

Make the head/bodice with paper clay over the foil-covered Styrofoam ball as instructed in the Techniques section except use paper clay rolled to 1/2″ thickness. Add a coil at the bottom of the neck to help hold the cloth body on.

Cut out the add-ons from paper clay rolled 1/2″ thick. Blend them into the head with sculpting tools and fingers dipped in water.

Make any additions or subtractions of clay. When you're satisfied, set the head aside to dry, then sand it carefully. Seal with two coats of gesso.

Paint the head with two coats of white. Paint the lips red, the eyes blue, the eyebrows and lashes black. Paint the facial designs with turquoise.

The wig is made of black English straight mohair. Measure the mohair to fit the head, place it between two pieces of wax paper, and sew the center seam. Glue it to the head.

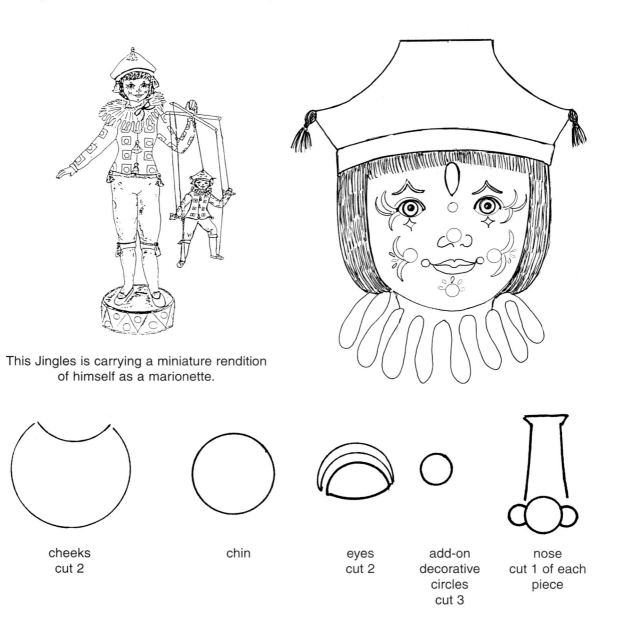

This Jingles is carrying a miniature rendition of himself as a marionette.

cheeks
cut 2

chin

eyes
cut 2

add-on
decorative
circles
cut 3

nose
cut 1 of each
piece

24" POLCINELLA

MATERIALS

paper clay or papier mâché
3¹⁵⁄₁₆″ Styrofoam oval for head armature
aluminum foil (4″ x 12″)
brown small curl mohair for wig
fabric and stuffing for cloth body (Polcinella
   cloth body pattern on page 128)
costume
Note: I used felt for the body and costume

cheeks
cut 2

ears
cut 2

This figure has a felt body with papier mâché head/neck, hands, and shoes. He has a brown mohair wig and brown sparkling painted eyes. I've always been fascinated by character dolls and love to create my own. I used a Polcinella paper doll for inspiration. The original Polcinella was invented by an actor in the early 1600s. The name means "little chicken," which fits the personality of the fictional character—strutting and squawking. The character became popular and was imitated as "Punch" in London.

Mix instant papier mâché and roll it to 1/2˝ thick. Fill a small bowl with water to rinse off tools and fingers as you work (papier mâché can be very sticky).

Cut out the pieces to fit around the foil covered head armature. Lightly pat it on the head. If it slides off, you've added too much water when mixing the mâché and need to add a little dry mâché to the mixture. Smooth the mâché with sculpting tools.

Use the photographs and drawings for the add-ons. Start by adding a piece for the forehead, then add the nose, ears, cheeks, eyes, coil lips, and eyelids. All the features on this character are very large. As you add each piece, use your fingers to gently push and mold the add-on piece into the existing mâché. Use your fingers and thumbs to push the coil eyebrows down over each eye, leaving a ridge over each eye.

Blend cheeks into each side and up. Make two ovals for the eyes and smooth the edges all around the eyes with your fingers and a sculpting tool.

Add a piece for the bridge of the nose and the three circles for the nostrils. Smooth and blend each piece. With your thumbs, push in on either side of the nose bridge and push in and up to create a nose bridge.

With your thumbs, push in gently under each eye and smooth out toward the side of the cheek, come down and round out the cheek. The clown has a big smile so his cheeks will be up on each side of his lips with smile lines on each side of his smile. Use the orange stick to poke in two holes for nostrils and dimples in his chin and cheeks.

Use a sculpting tool to enlarge the center of his big smile. You can make teeth cut from cardboard and fit them into the lips. Push the cardboard teeth into the mâché and let them dry. Use the side of the sculpting tool to press about 1/8˝ deep smile lines on his face.

Add more mâché if needed. After the ears are pressed into the sides of the head, study the head and see what extra detail you want to add. Remember, this is a character figure, so even if it comes out really rough looking it will still be interesting. Let dry.

Instant papier mâché has been cut into strips and covers the armature. Circles and coils are added to build up the features. I added a rectangle for the forehead.

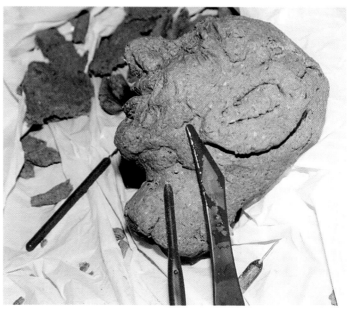

Smooth the large nose and blend it into the mâché. Add a large coil for the mouth and shape it into a big smile. Add the large ears.

Polcinella with all his features smoothed. Notice the lines in the forehead and around his eyes. His ears are large, his nose protrudes, his chin sticks out, and his smile is big. I made nostrils by inserting the round end of the detail sculpting into the nose.

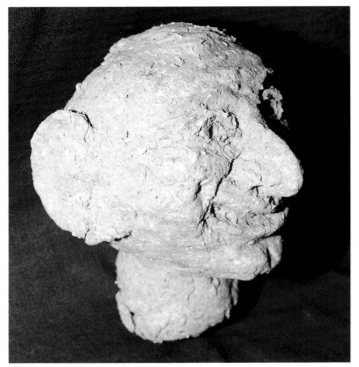

The finished head takes at least three days to dry in ideal drying temperatures. I didn't sand

this piece because the wrinkles add to the character. When dry, seal with about four coats of gesso to fill in any rough spots. Now it's ready to paint.

Paint with two coats of flesh paint. Draw in the features with a pencil before painting with a small pointed brush. Paint the eyes white, then add blue or brown irises and black pupils. For the mouth, mix a dot of red with 1/4 teaspoon of flesh paint. Paint the teeth white.

For the nose and checks, mix 1/2 teaspoon of flesh with a drop of red and mix well. Use two 1/2″ flat brushes, one with cheek color and one with flesh. Brush on the cheek color and blend in all around the edges with flesh paint.

Mix a drop of brown acrylic paint with two teaspoons acrylic satin varnish. Paint a thin coat around the eyes, nose, and face lines and dimples, then wipe lightly with a damp soft cloth. The flesh color will show through and the wrinkles and lines in the face will be accentuated by the color that remains. This also adds shadows around the eyes, nose, and ears. If too much remains, wipe off again until you like the look. If you wipe off too much, apply more. The glazing is only done on character faces, not on children or ladies.

Adding hair ▮

Measure the length and width of the head and cut a piece of mohair to fit. Place the mohair between two pieces of wax paper and sew the center part on the sewing machine. Glue the mohair wig to the head. Let the glue dry overnight. Fluff and style with your fingers and spray with hair spray.

For the beard, start at the chin line and brush on glue and work upward, adding pieces of precut mohair. You can make the beard any length you want. Eyebrows can be painted on or you can glue on small strands of mohair starting from the right and working left. After the glue is dry, brush with fingers and a hair prong and trim.

Cut two hands out of papier mâché 1/2″ thick. Use sculpting tools to shape the fingers, palms, and wrists. Add more mâché if necessary to round out the fingers, wrists, and palms. Let the hands dry over a 1/2″ wood dowel to give them a slight curve. You can curve one more than the other. When the mâché has dried, seal with two coats of gesso, let dry, and paint with the same skin tone as the face. When the paint is dry, apply varnish.

For the wooden shoes, cut the pieces out of papier mâché 1/2″ thick. After you've sewn the cloth body, cover the feet with plastic wrap and wrap the papier mâché pieces around the feet to shape the shoes. Smooth in all the seams and let it dry on the foot. Once the mâché is dry, remove the shoe and seal with gesso. Let dry and paint. When the paint has dried, apply varnish.

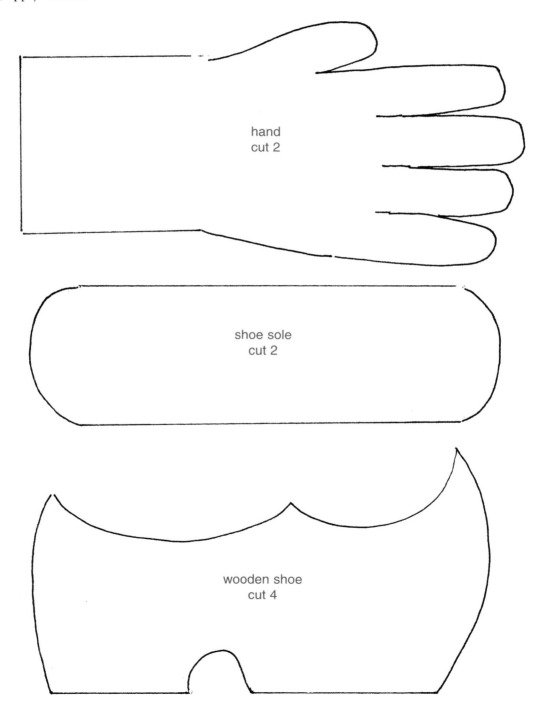

hand
cut 2

shoe sole
cut 2

wooden shoe
cut 4

20" OLD CHRIS

MATERIALS

paper clay or papier mâché (8 oz.)
2½" Styrofoam ball for head armature
aluminum foil (4" x 12")
taper candles for leg armatures
taper candles for arm armatures
white crepe wool for hair
wire to form body armature inside cloth body
fabric and stuffing for cloth body (Old
   Chris cloth body pattern on page 132)
costume (pattern on page 153)

Old Chris is based on the Father Christmas of Great Britain, a red-faced, holly-crowned rakish fellow who rode a goat and blessed fruit trees. He would take a drink from a cup of wassail and throw the remainder at the tree's roots to insure a good harvest in the year to come.

Refer to the directions in the Techniques section to sculpt the paper clay face, lower arms, and lower legs over armatures. Add facial features with paper clay add-ons

smoothed and blended into the head. Press wrinkles in the forehead, cheeks, and chin.

Paint the face, hands, and feet with flesh acrylic paint. Let dry. Mix dark flesh and varnish in equal parts. Brush around the eyes, nose, forehead, and into all the wrinkles. Wipe off immediately with a soft cloth. All the wrinkles and shadows will be accentuated.

I used a needlepoint tool to press lines in the hands to suggest fingers. Press the fingertips with an orange stick to form fingernails. Do the same thing to the feet.

When you're satisfied with the sculpting, let the paper clay dry completely. Sand if necessary and seal with two coats of gesso. Refer to the photo and paint the paper clay pieces. Seal with varnish and add the hair, mustache, and beard. Glue strands of hair on the head individually. Glue the paper clay head, hands, and legs to the cloth body.

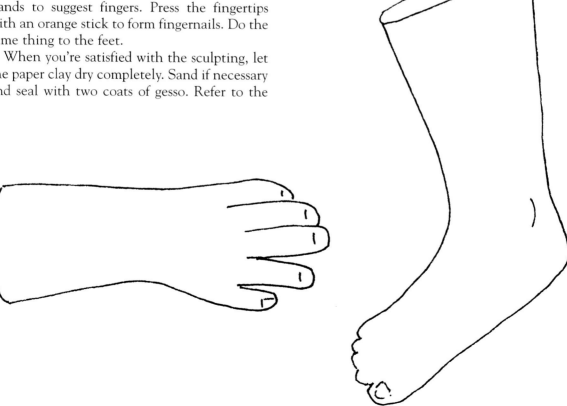

To make your own add-ons for Old Chris, trace the drawing below. Cut into the following sections: forehead; nose (roll three clay balls); two eye shapes; two cheek shapes; one chin; a circle for ears; coils for eyelids and lips. Place on paper clay and cut out.

back of head

Use 3″ long strands of wool. Glue three strands to each circle in the drawing. Start at the bottom and work up. Do the head and then the beard. Pre-cut all the strands.

BILLY GOATS

MATERIALS

Paper clay or papier mâché (2 lbs.)
2″ x 9″ x 3″ Styrofoam rectangle for body
   armature
4 taper candles for leg armatures
10″ taper candle for head and neck armature
Heavyweight aluminum foil
Heavyweight watercolor paper for ears and
   hooves
12″ x 14″ piece of wool roving for hair

These goats are 10″ tall and 14″ long. Each one will have its own individual look. No two ever come out exactly alike.

How to make the goat armature ■

Refer to the diagrams on page 101. Cut a piece of foil 12″ x 10″ and fold in half. Wrap the 6″ x 10″ folded piece of foil around a 10″ taper candle. Remove the foil from the candle and shape it as shown for the neck and head. The neck should protrude 2″ above the body and the head should be 3″ long.

Cut a piece of aluminum foil 14″x 12″ and fold it in half. Place the Styrofoam rectangle in the center of the foil and wrap foil around the Styrofoam. Tape the foil neck and head piece to the Styrofoam body piece.

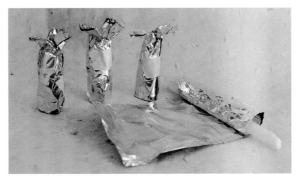

To make the leg armatures, cut four 12″ x 4″ pieces of aluminum foil. Wrap a piece of foil around the narrow end of each taper candle to form the legs. Press and sculpt the foil around the candle. Secure the seam with masking tape. Remove the foil from the candle. Each leg should be 4″ long and about 4″ in circumference. Cut each leg 1″ down from the top on each side of leg. Spread one piece of foil to the left and one piece to the right. One piece will be glued under the body and one piece glued to the outside of the body. Use masking tape to tape the legs to the body.

Tape all the armature pieces together. This armature is ready for the papier mâché covering.

Mix 2 lbs. of papier mâché in a large plastic bag. Knead until it's firm and well blended. If it's too dry, add more water and mix. Roll it out in the plastic bag until the mâché is about 1/2″ thick. Place a piece of wax paper under the goat armature. Cut the mâché into 3″ x 4″ pieces and place each piece carefully on the armature. The papier mâché is very sticky and adheres easily to the armature. Do the body first, then the legs. Wrap a piece of mâché around each leg and smooth and blend it together at the seam. Press gently so the mâché sticks to the aluminum foil.

Cover the head with mâché and use the round end tool to press and smooth the mâché. Make a line of separation for the goat's mouth. Use your fingertip to press in the nostrils.

Add the cutouts (page 102) for the eyes, the piece for the nose, and two coil eyelids. Add a rolled coil about 1/2″ round to the top of the head and insert the two horns (see below).

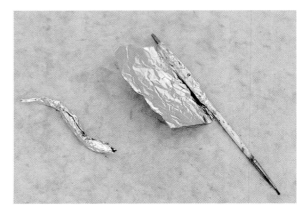

To make the horns, cut two 3″ x 4″ pieces of foil and roll each one around the handle of a 20/0 paint brush handle. Slip the foil off the handle and shape so the horn is wider on the bottom and narrow at the tip. Insert the horns in the clay on the top of the goat's head.

Cut four hooves (pattern on page 101) out of heavyweight watercolor paper. Dip each hoof in water and blot dry with a paper towel. Glue the back of the paper and wrap around the base of each leg, overlapping in the back. Tie with thread until the glue is dry.

Cut two ears (pattern on page 101) from heavyweight watercolor paper. Fold the tabs down and fold in half on the center line. Unfold and apply glue to the tab. Glue ears in place on the head.

Close up of legs and hooves.

This shows the goat covered with papier mâché with the horns, ears, and hooves in place. Cover each horn with 1/4″ thick mâché, making the horn wider at the bottom and narrower at each tip. Smooth and add extra detail if needed, then set aside to dry. Make sure the mâché is completely dry before sealing with gesso.

When the mâché is dry, seal with two coats of gesso and paint with white paint. Now you're ready to paint the face. Refer to the photo when painting the face, or choose your own colors. Pencil in the features before painting. I painted gray around the eyes, nose, and mouth, then wiped it off. This leaves a nice shadow. I painted yellow eyes with black pupils. When all the paint dries, apply two coats of varnish.

Adding the wool roving ▐■

When the varnish is completely dry, add the wool roving. I covered one goat with gray and one with white. Measure the goat from neck to tail and a cut a piece to fit over the goat's back and sides long enough to cover half of the legs. Cut small pieces to glue on the head, around the horns, face, and beard.

Brush on glue from the neck to the tail along the center of the back, under the chin, and around the horns. Brush glue around the upper 2″ of each leg. Pull the roving apart and glue it to the goat's back. Pull a small piece of roving for each leg (about 3″ x 4″) and wrap it around each leg, making sure the pulled edges are placed on the vertical. You will need to pull it down with your fingers and gently comb the wool down with a fork or hair prong. Some of the roving will pull out as you comb, just save it to glue around the head and neck and to wrap and curl around the horns as shown in the drawings. Brush the roving on the back with your fingers, over the upper legs, and around the ankles, making sure the hooves are visible.

Spray non-aerosol hair spray on the wool, pushing it in with your fingers to form waves or curls. Refer to the photo when shaping the wool. Wrap with thread to hold the wool in place and spray again with hair spray. After the spray dries, remove the thread.

Pull a piece of roving for the beard and glue it to the chin. Spray with hair spray. I left the gray wool roving straight. The white goat is covered with white wool roving.

How to assemble the head, neck, and body.

Neck: Wrap a 6″ x 10″ folded piece of foil around the candle.

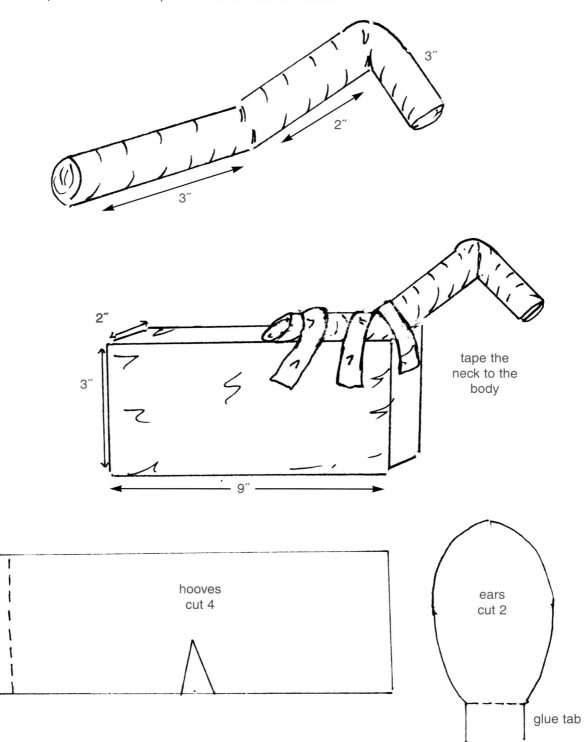

3″

2″

3″

2″

3″

tape the
neck to the
body

9″

hooves
cut 4

ears
cut 2

glue tab

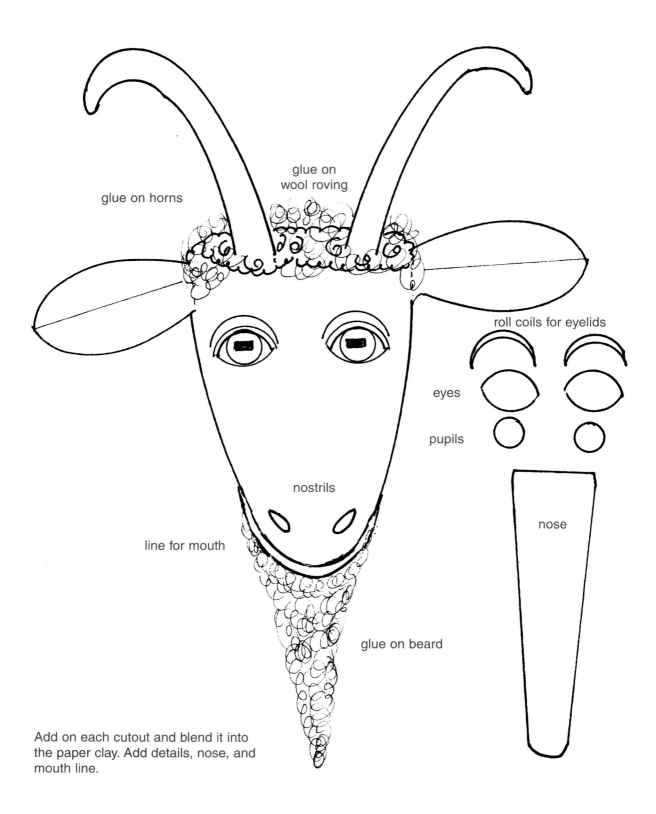

glue on horns

glue on
wool roving

roll coils for eyelids

eyes

pupils

nostrils

nose

line for mouth

glue on beard

Add on each cutout and blend it into
the paper clay. Add details, nose, and
mouth line.

For the ears, fold the tabs down and fold in half on the center line. Unfold and apply glue to the tab.

Glue the tabs and press the ears on side of the head.

26" RABBIT

MATERIALS

5 lb. instant papier mâché
3 liter plastic soda bottle for body armature
5″ x 3¾″ Styrofoam oval for head armature
taper candle for neck armature
aluminum foil
masking tape
cardboard for legs and ears
costume (pattern on page 154)

Roll aluminum foil around a large candle to shape the neck armature.

Remove the candle, cut a hole in the Styrofoam egg and insert 2″ of the foil neck into it. Insert the other end of the neck armature into the soda bottle. The neck should be 4″ long (the distance between the head and the soda bottle).

Cut out two cardboard ears (pattern on page 107) and insert them into the Styrofoam head armature.

Cut out two cardboard upper leg sections (pattern on page 109) and two cardboard lower leg sections (pattern on page 110).

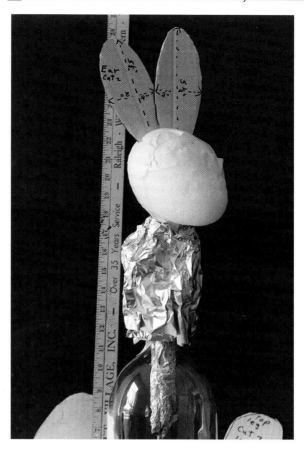

Wrap more foil around the neck.

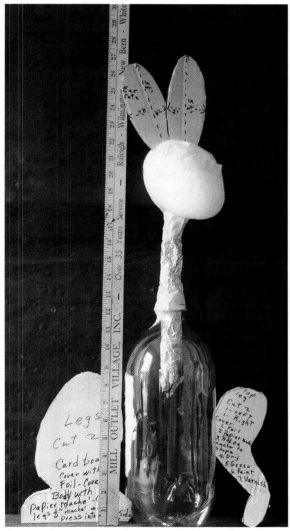

Insert the cardboard ears in the Styrofoam head armature which is attached to the foil neck armature in the soda bottle. The cardboard leg pieces aren't attached yet.

Cover the entire figure from the neck down with foil. Secure the foil with masking tape.

Mix the full 5 lbs. of papier mâché in a plastic bag according to the manufacturer's directions. With the bag on a hard surface, knead until the water is well blended into the mâché and it feels firm. Flatten and spread the mâché evenly in the bag and use a rolling pin to roll it out to 1/2″ thick. Cut open the bag and use the pizza cutter to cut the mâché into 2″ x 4″ pieces. It's best to work with instant mâché the first day it's mixed because it sticks easily and quickly to the armature and spreads smoothly.

Cover the entire rabbit armature with mâché pieces. Start with the lower legs and work up, doing one side at a time. Do the back next and then the front. Cover all the way up to the neck with 1/2″ mâché. Add extra mâché on the feet and at the base. Continue adding, smoothing, and tucking pieces into areas where the legs join the body. I used a small rubber spatula to smooth the mâché as I added each piece.

I work rather quickly, covering one side in about an hour. Then I take a break and do the other side. Add more mâché at the bottom, adding weight at the base so it won't tip over.

Cover the head and ears with aluminum foil and secure with masking tape. Cover the upper and lower leg sections with aluminum foil and tape them to the body as shown.

Cover the head with mâché and use 1/4″ thick pieces to cover the ears. Fill in and round out areas on the legs, stomach, and feet.

Cut out the add-ons from 1/4″ thick mâché and blend them into the face.

Add texture with a large salad fork and a smaller dessert fork. Gently press the fork at the base of the feet on top of each leg and all over the rabbit. Use a smaller fork on the face, ears, and over the stomach area. Pull the fork upward in a combing motion. You can add a little or a lot of texture. Add a tail of crumpled foil and cover with 1/2″ mâché. Press the tail into the back between the hind legs.

Let the mâché dry completely. My rabbit took three days to dry by placing it outside in the sun during the day and inside over the heat vent at night. Tap it with a wooden dowel and it will sound almost like wood when it is dry. When dry, seal with two coats of gesso and paint the entire rabbit with white, gray, or brown acrylic. Paint the eyes pink and brown and the nose and mouth and inside of ears a light pink. Outline the mouth, eyes, and nose with brown. When you're satisfied with the result, seal with two coats of acrylic varnish.

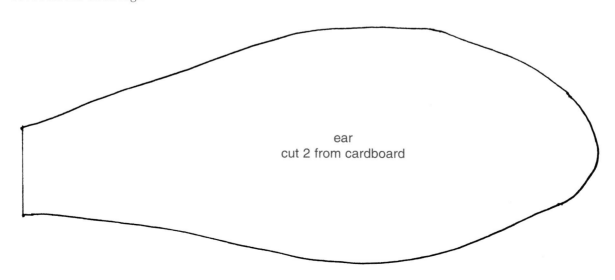

ear
cut 2 from cardboard

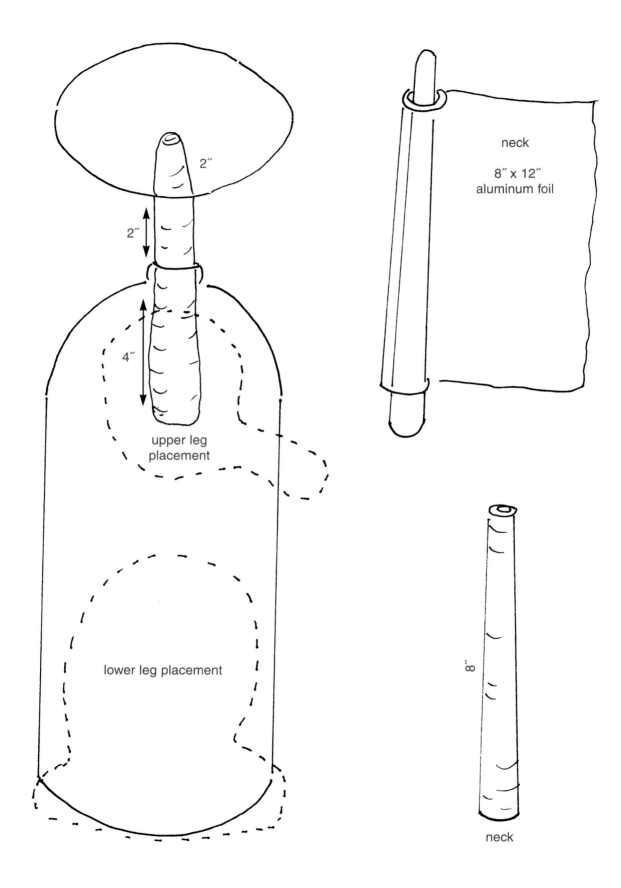

2″

2″

4″

upper leg
placement

lower leg placement

neck

8″ x 12″
aluminum foil

8″

neck

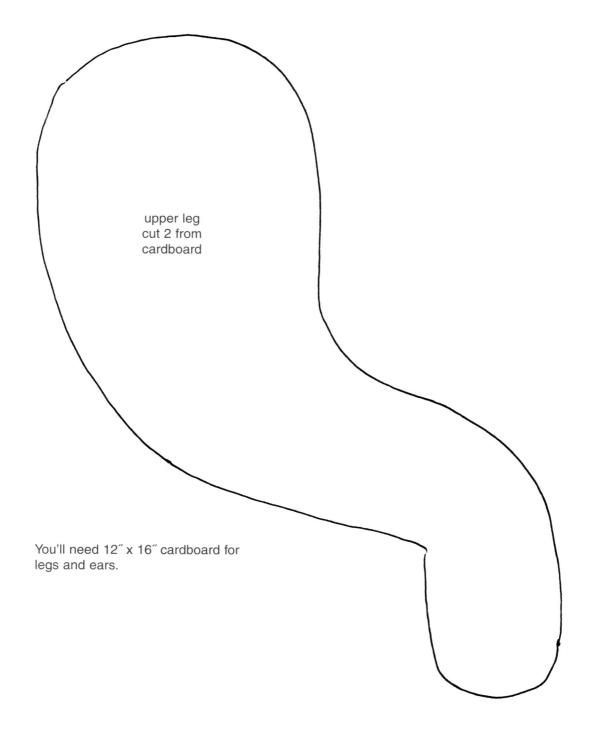

upper leg
cut 2 from
cardboard

You'll need 12˝ x 16˝ cardboard for
legs and ears.

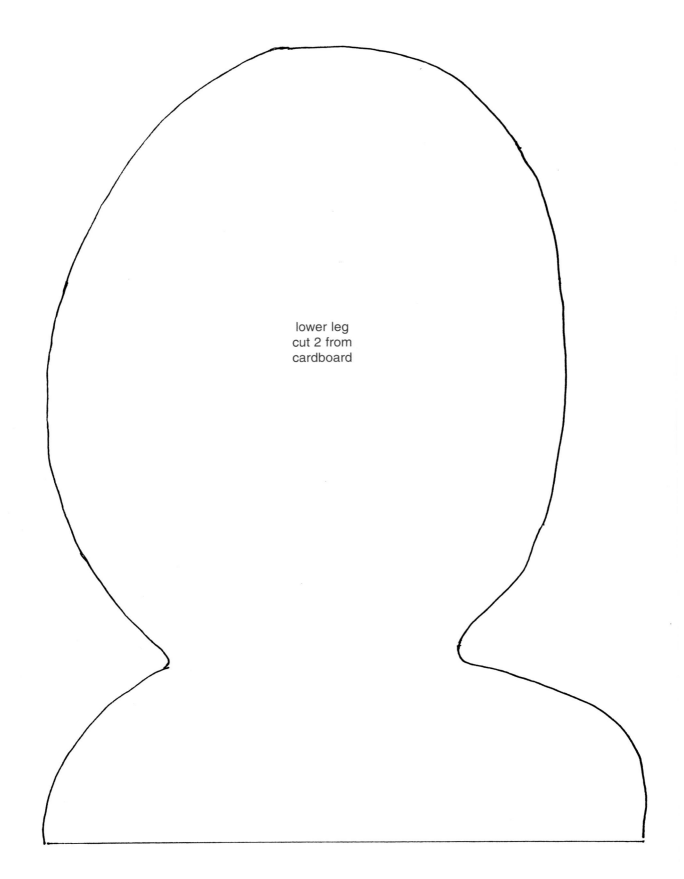

lower leg
cut 2 from
cardboard

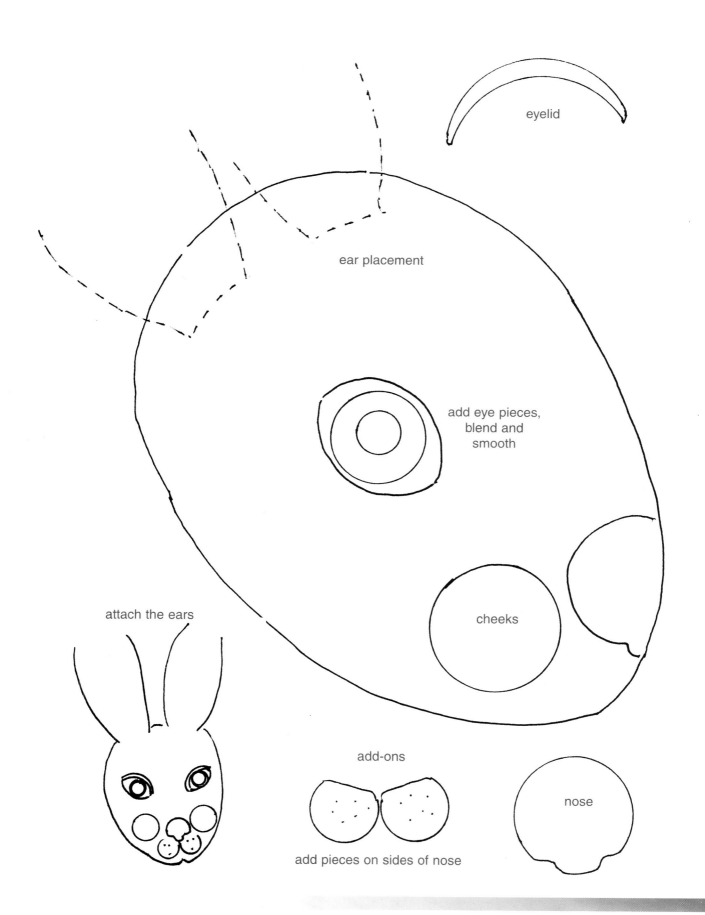

eyelid

ear placement

add eye pieces,
blend and
smooth

cheeks

attach the ears

add-ons

nose

add pieces on sides of nose

Gallery

Swagman is an original creation inspired by the Australian folk song, "Waltzing Matilda." His hands, head, and feet are papier mâché and his hair is wool.

This 36˝ *Country Santa* was made by pressing paper clay into one of my original plaster molds.

Here are a few figures I've made over the years. These figures illustrate how truly diverse paper clay and papier mâché are. You are limited only by your imagination!

I made this 30˝ *Santa* in 1984 using papier mâché.

Gentleman Beetle Marionette is hand-sculpted paper clay over wood.

Gallery

Towering over Polcinella is the 50″ St. Nicholas hand-sculpted of papier mâché.

Bearing Gifts is a 17″ Santa figure hand-sculpted with paper clay head, hands, and feet. This figure was donated to the Association of Retarded Citizens auction.

To make this 33″ Angel, I hand-sculpted the head, bodice, and hands from paper clay and made her hair from twine. She received a Best of Show award in 1994.

This beautiful 53″ St. Nicholas figure is regal in burgandy velvet with gold ribbons and bows.

Gallery

The Lord of Misrule is a one-of-a-kind 33˝ figure hand-sculpted from papier mâché.

Riding on a ceramic elephant, this 17˝ *St. Nick* is made from paper clay pressed in a plaster mold.

These antique *Santas* stand 17˝ tall. They are made from paper clay pressed in my original plaster mold.

Alice is made from paper clay. She's standing in my garden with my original 33˝ white cotton rabbit.

About the Author

Doris Rockwell Gottilly is a multi-media artist currently working with papier mâché acrylics and fabric. She specializes in sculptures depicting a wide-range of characters, from *Beauty and the Beast* to *Olde World Father Christmas*, using history and folk tales as inspiration.

Her extensive research, combined with natural talent, bring remarkable authenticity to her creations. She designs, creates marionettes, and stages marionette shows. Sculpting, mold making, painting, designing, pattern making, and sewing as well as the eye of the artist are some of the skills she uses to create her figures and to teach doll sculpting.

She has exhibited her figure sculptures in art and craft shows throughout the country and has won multitudes of awards. She is the author of the book, *Creative Dollmaking*, and many magazine articles in *Doll Reader*, *Dollmaking*, and others. Her 50″ Old World Father Christmas appeared on the cover of *Country Sampler* magazine in 1993.

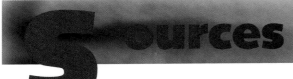

Most of the supplies needed for the projects in this book are available at local art and craft supply stores and fabric shops.

Activa Products, Inc.
P.O. Box 1296
Marshall, TX 75670-0023
instant papier mâché

Aleene's
85 Industrial Way
Buellton CA 93427
(805) 688-7339
super-tacky glue

All Cooped Up
560 S. State #1
Orem, UT 84058
(801)226-1517)
curly crepe wool

Bell Ceramics, Inc.
P.O. Box 120127
Clermont, FL 34712
(352) 394-2175
plaster molds, dollmaking supplies, brushes, wigs, mohair

Craft Catalog
P.O. Box 1069
Reynoldsburg, OH
(800) 777-1442
acrylic paints, gesso, varnish, polyester fiberfill, wire, doll hair, wool, papier mâché

Craft King
P.O. Box 90637
Lakeland, FL 33804
(800) 769-9494
Styrofoam, papier mâché, brushes, acrylic paints 2 oz. bottles, gesso, varnish, flexible bead armatures, papier based air dry clay

Creative Paperclay®
1800 S. Robertson Blvd.,
Ste. 907
Los Angeles, CA 90035
(310) 839-0466
paper clay

Dick Blick Art Materials
P.O. Box 1267
Galesburg, IL 61402-1267
(800) 828-4548
paints, brushes, disposable gloves

Dollspart Supply
8000 Cooper Ave., Bldg. 28
Glendale, NY 11385
(800) 336-3655
dollmaking supplies, wigs, mohair, paint brushes, eyes, teeth

Fleece and Unicorn
Seventh Avenue Center
123 West 7th Ave. Ste. #102
Stillwater, OK 74074-4029
(405) 377-7105
yarns and fibers for doll hair, all traditional hair colors and textures of wool, mohair, loose washed fleece

Floracraft,
Ludington, MI 49431
(616) 845-5127
Styrofoam eggs and balls

Jerry's Artarama
117 South 2nd St.
P.O. Box 1105
New Hyde Park, NY 11040
(516) 328-6633
paper clay, papier mâché, sculpting tools, brushes, acrylic paints, and supplies

Kemper Mfg. Co.
P.O. Box 696
Chicho, CA 91710
(909) 627-6193
dollmaking supplies, wigs, brushes

One & Only Creations
P.O. Box 2730
Napa, CA 94558
hair and mini curls

Seeley's
P.O. Box 669
9 River St.
Oneonta, NY 13820
(800) 433-1191
plaster molds, dollmaking supplies, brushes, wigs, mohair

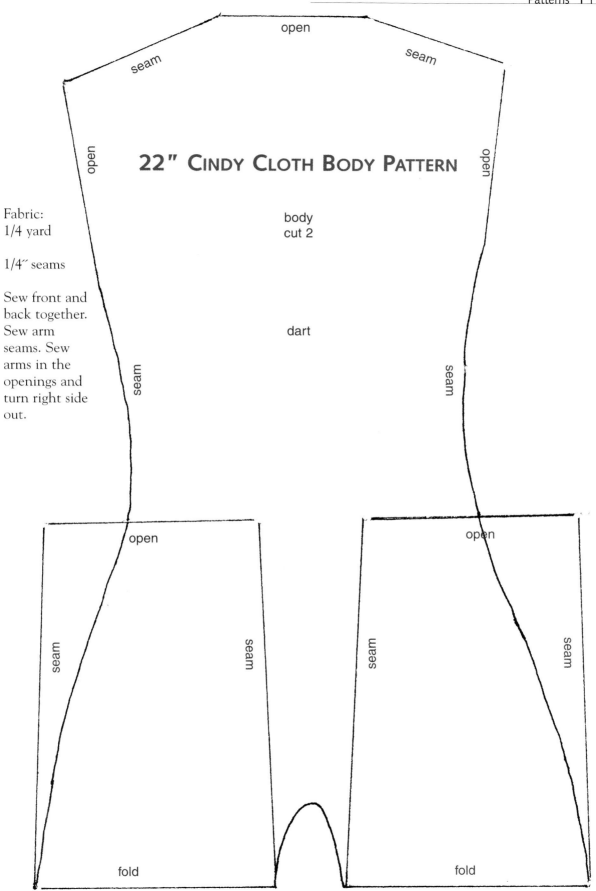

open

seam   seam

open   open

22" CINDY CLOTH BODY PATTERN

Fabric:
1/4 yard

1/4˝ seams

Sew front and
back together.
Sew arm
seams. Sew
arms in the
openings and
turn right side
out.

body
cut 2

dart

seam   seam

open   open

seam   seam   seam   seam

fold   fold

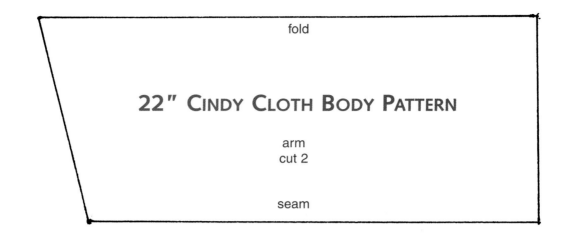

22" CINDY CLOTH BODY PATTERN

arm
cut 2

seam

fold

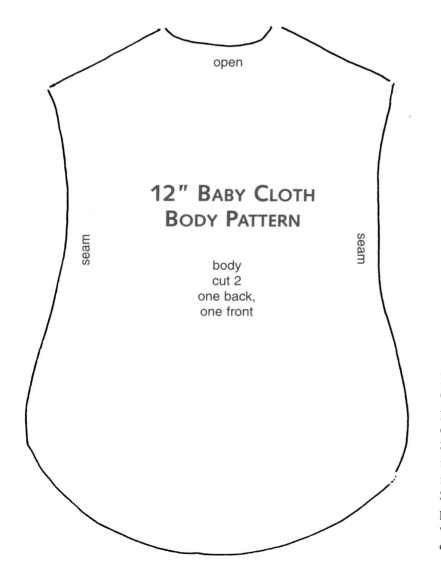

12" BABY CLOTH BODY PATTERN

open

seam

seam

body
cut 2
one back,
one front

sew dart
in back

Fabric: 8″ x 16″
Cut out the cloth body pattern as shown. Sew a dart in the back piece. Sew all 1/4″ seams, leaving openings for the stuffing and paper clay pieces. Sew the front and back pieces together all the way around from neck opening to neck opening.

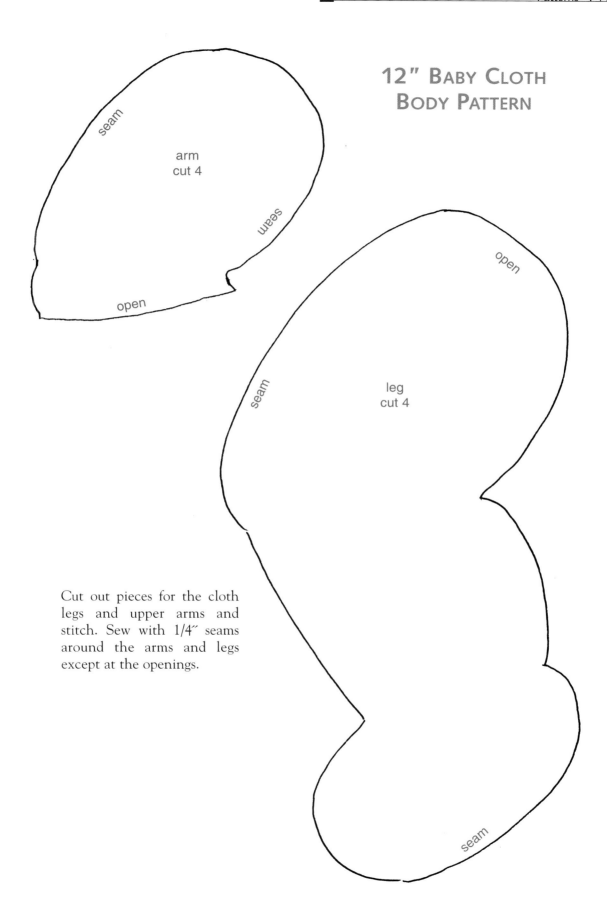

12" BABY CLOTH BODY PATTERN

arm
cut 4

seam

seam

open

leg
cut 4

open

seam

seam

Cut out pieces for the cloth legs and upper arms and stitch. Sew with 1/4″ seams around the arms and legs except at the openings.

12" CHILD CLOTH BODY PATTERN (USED FOR YURI, KATE, KEISHA, YOUNG PRINCE)

Fabric: 8˝ x 16˝
To make the cloth body, cut out as directed on the pattern. Sew darts on the front and back. Sew the side seams and leg seams, then turn right side out. Stuff with cotton batting. Glue the paper clay head/neck and arm and leg sections in the cloth body. Sew with 1/4˝ seams.

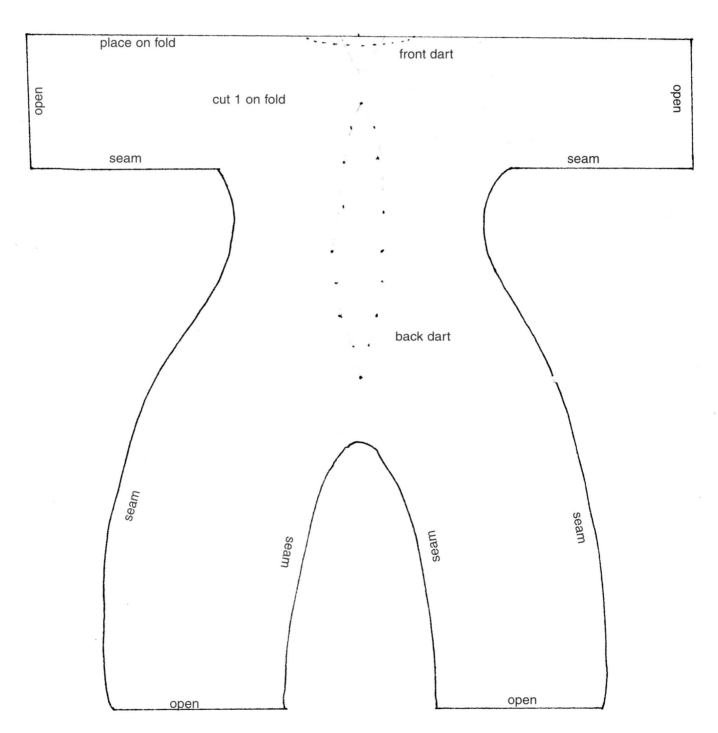

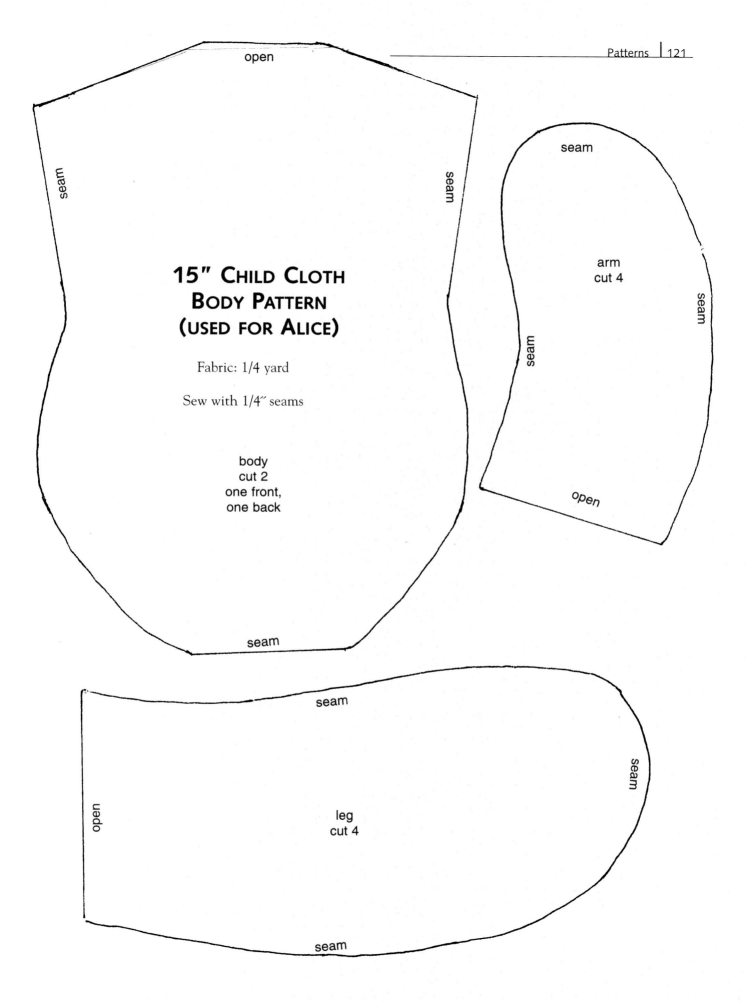

open

seam

seam

15" CHILD CLOTH BODY PATTERN (USED FOR ALICE)

Fabric: 1/4 yard

Sew with 1/4″ seams

body
cut 2
one front,
one back

seam

seam

arm
cut 4

seam

seam

open

seam

open

leg
cut 4

seam

seam

Fabric: 1/4 yard muslin, cotton Place patterns on fabric. Cut out each piece as instructed on the patterns. Sew with 1/4″ seams (when making Tasha, sew with 5/8″ seams). Sew the arm and leg seams. Turn right side out, fold 1/4″ of fabric under at the arm openings and apply glue to the upper edge of the paper clay arm and insert it in the arm opening. Keep pressure on the arm and fabric until the glue dries and the cloth and paper clay are securely

open for stuffing

seam

seam

17″ Cloth Body (used for Scarlett Melanie Beauty Queen Elizabeth I China Doll English Doll Tasha)

seam

seam

back cut 1

open

open

seam

seam

front cut 2

seam

seam

joined. Glue the legs into the leg opening in fabric in the same way. When the glue is dry, stuff the cloth arm and leg.

Sew the front seam of the body. Place the front and back pieces together, right sides in, and sew up the side seams and shoulders, leaving openings at the neck, arms, and legs. Turn right side out. Sew arms and legs to the body as shown in the drawing. Stuff the body firmly and apply tacky glue to the neck of the finished doll head. Insert the neck into the body and baste around the neck with heavy-duty thread. Pull the thread tightly and tie in a knot.

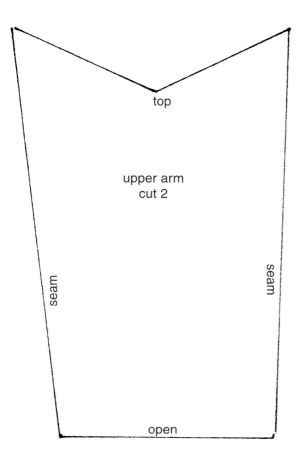

upper arm
cut 2

seam

seam

top

open

Fold arms and legs in half and sew the seam.

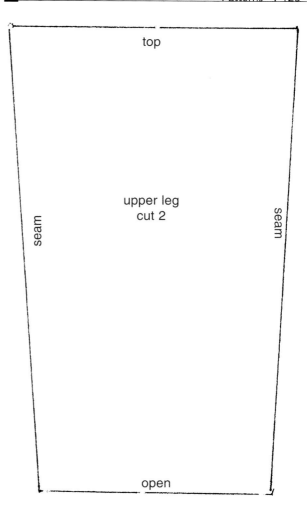

top

seam

seam

upper leg
cut 2

open

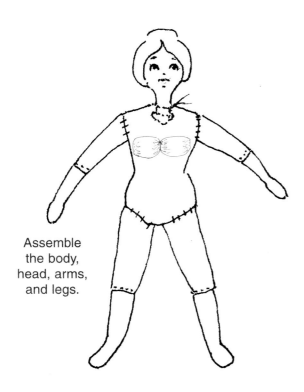

Assemble
the body,
head, arms,
and legs.

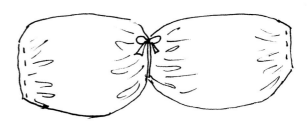

If you wish to make a doll with an extra padded bust, add a lace undergarment. Make the undergarment from a piece of lace, 3″ x 3″. Fold the lace to 1½″ x 3″ and sew a seam opposite the fold. Turn right side out and tie the center with a 1/4″ silk ribbon. Stuff each side and sew up each side, gathering as you sew. Sew on the doll body at the bodice.

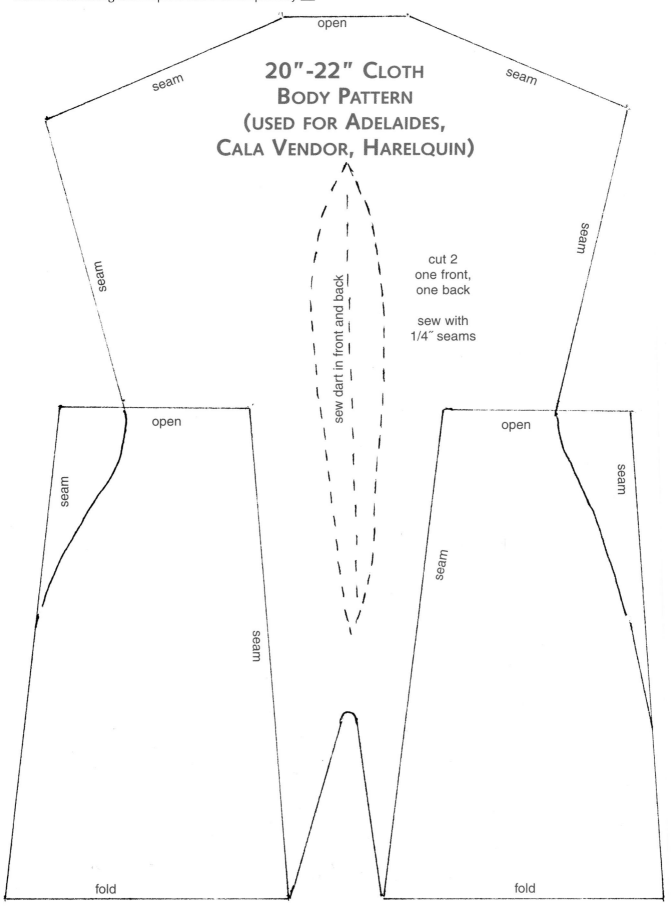

open

seam

seam

seam

seam

20"-22" CLOTH
BODY PATTERN
(USED FOR ADELAIDES,
CALA VENDOR, HARELQUIN)

sew dart in front and back

cut 2
one front,
one back

sew with
1/4″ seams

open

seam

open

seam

seam

seam

fold

fold

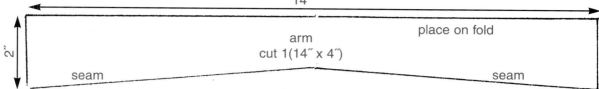

14″

2″

arm
cut 1(14″ x 4″)

place on fold

seam

seam

Fabric: 1/2 yard unbleached muslin, cotton chintz, or broadcloth. Measure the circumference of the paper clay arms and legs before cutting out the cloth body pattern. Each sculpture will vary in size. Make adjustments to the pattern to fit your individual sculpture. Sew the darts in the front and back. Hem the cloth arms and legs 1/4″ or sew lace as a finishing touch. Glue in the paper clay arms and legs.

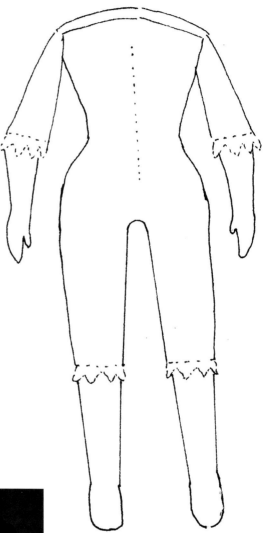

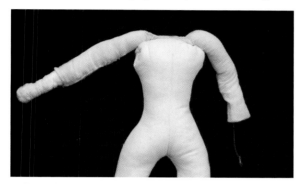

This photo shows a body that has been sewn and stuffed. A wire has been inserted through the arm tube prior to sewing the cloth arms across the bodice. This shows one arm wrapped with cotton batting tied with thread.

Left: Harlequin, Adelaide, and Cala Vendor all have bodies made from this basic body pattern. Cindy (in the hat) has her own body pattern to fit a flexible plastic armature. Each body is different and has been adjusted to fit the design of each doll. Harlequin is flexible and the seams have been made larger to slim the figure. Adelaide is full size with extra padding. Cindy is super slim. Cala Vendor has the full pattern with arms wired.

20" JINGLES
CLOTH BODY PATTERN

Fabric: 1/2 yard white felt

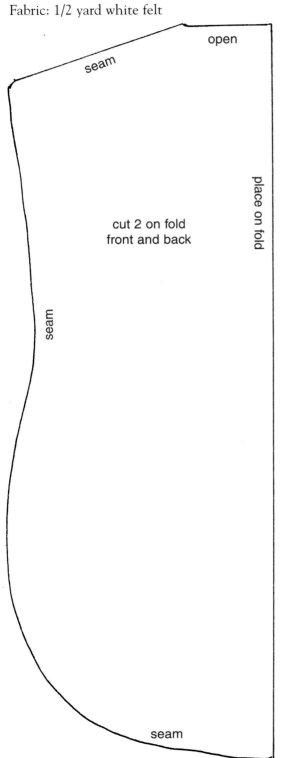

open

seam

cut 2 on fold
front and back

place on fold

seam

seam

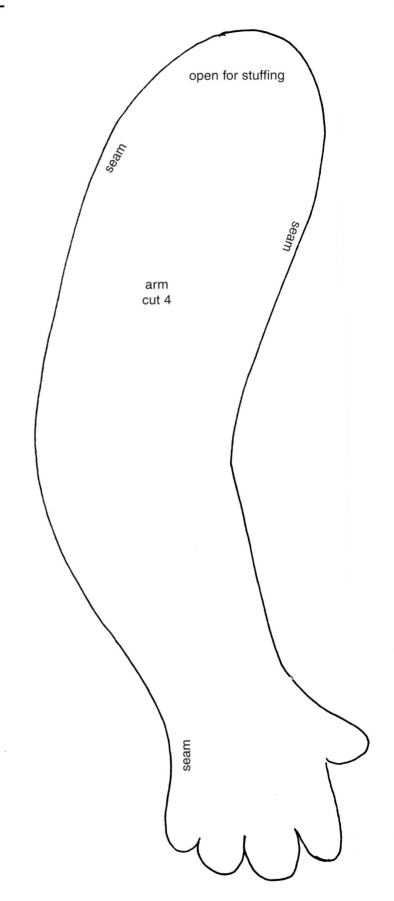

open for stuffing

seam

seam

arm
cut 4

seam

Sew the leg pieces together, leaving openings for turning and stuffing. Sew the sole to the bottom of the foot and turn right side out and stuff. Sew the arms and legs to the body by inserting a 5″ threaded needle through the arms and body and tying from right to left, then left to right, and tying firmly on each side. Firmly stuff all the cloth parts and sew up the openings by hand. Glue the paper clay head into the cloth body. Refer to the body assembly diagram for Polcinella on page 131.

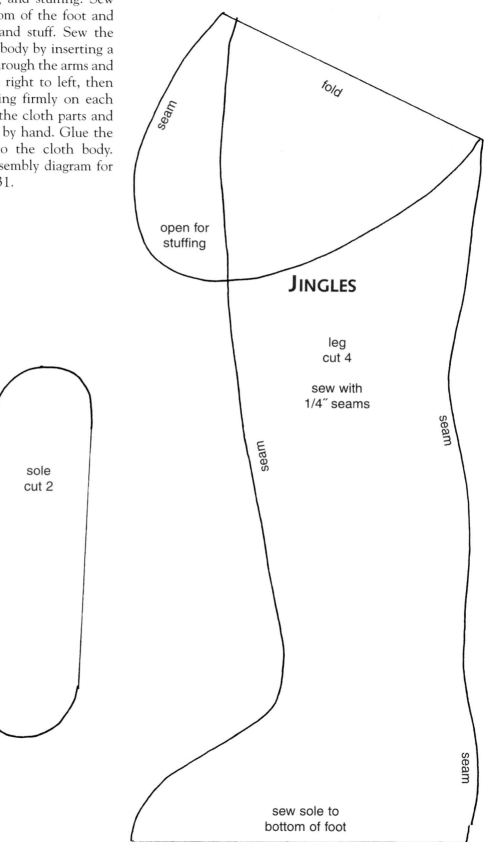

seam

fold

open for
stuffing

JINGLES

leg
cut 4

sew with
1/4″ seams

seam

seam

sole
cut 2

seam

sew sole to
bottom of foot

24" POLCINELLA
CLOTH BODY PATTERN

Fabric: 3/4 yard red
felt for body

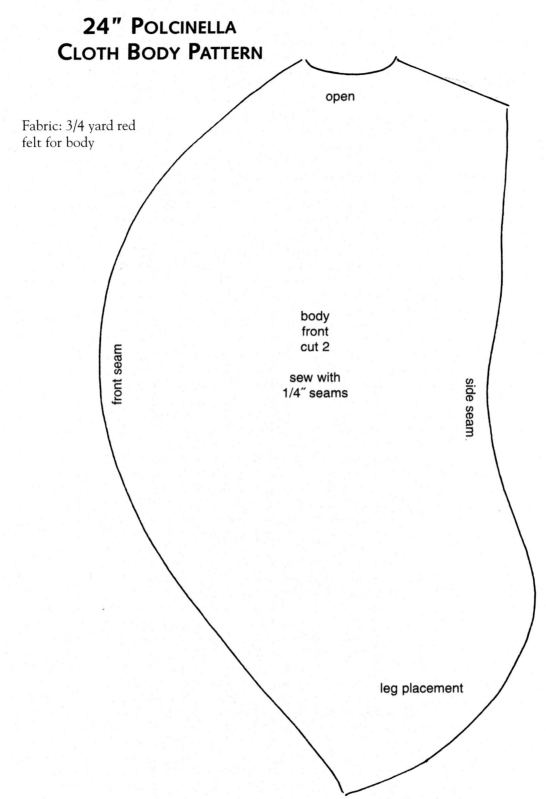

open

body
front
cut 2

sew with
1/4″ seams

front seam

side seam

leg placement

24" POLCINELLA
CLOTH BODY PATTERN

Sew the front seam, then the back seam. Sew the shoulders of the front and back body pieces together, leaving an opening at the neck. Sew the front to the back at the side seams. Turn right side out and stuff.

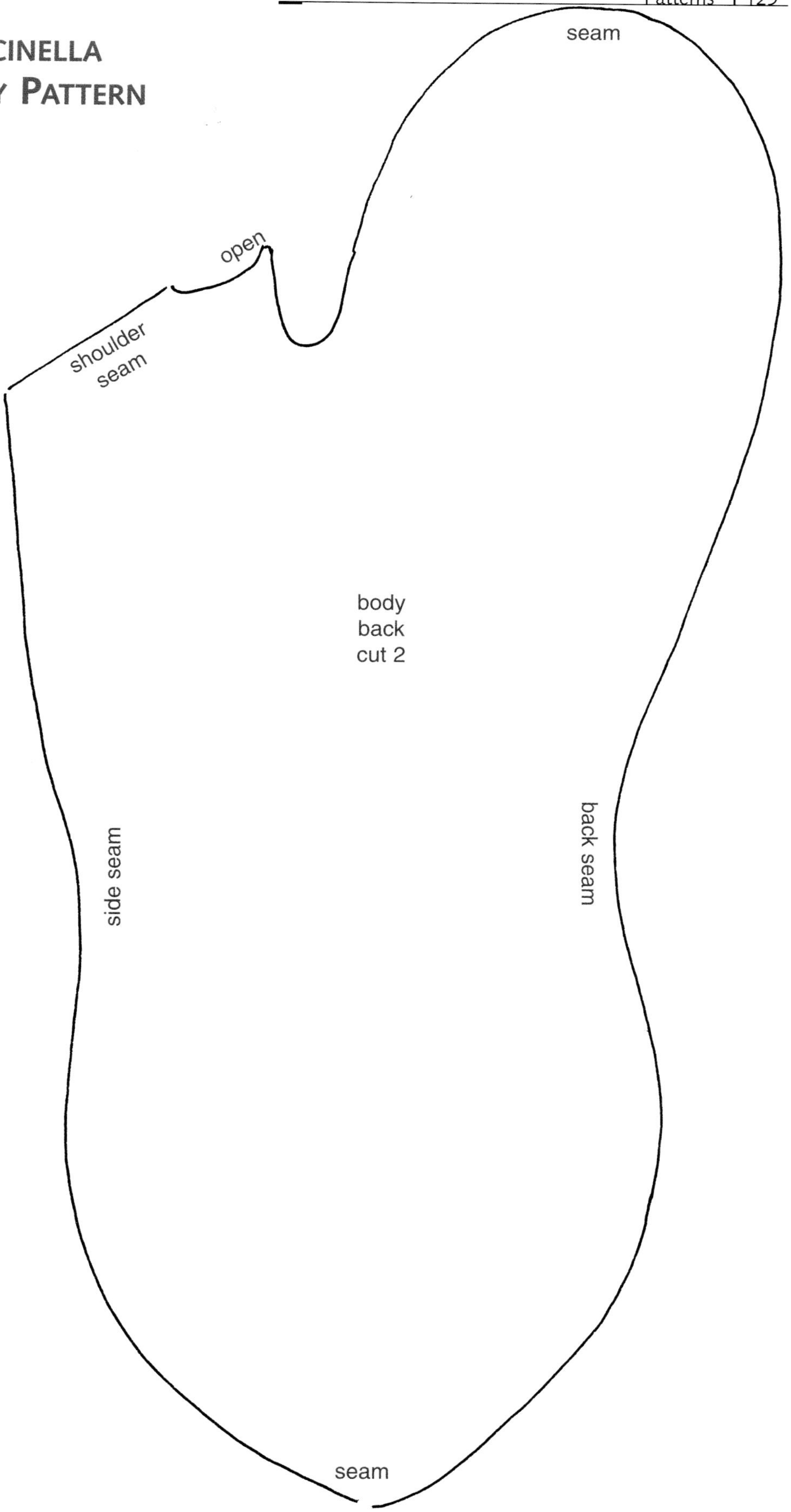

seam

open

shoulder seam

body
back
cut 2

side seam

back seam

seam

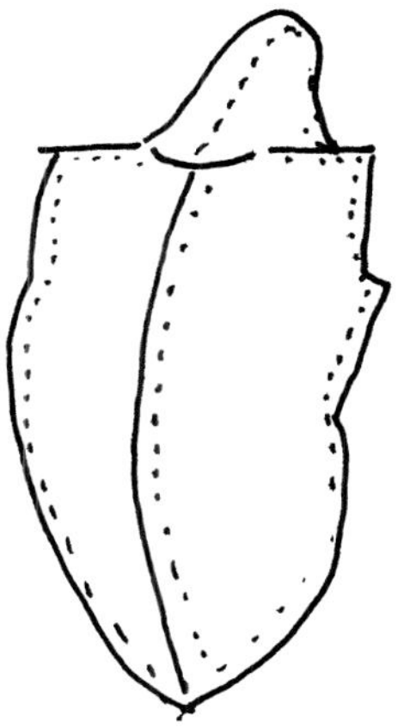

24" POLCINELLA CLOTH BODY PATTERN

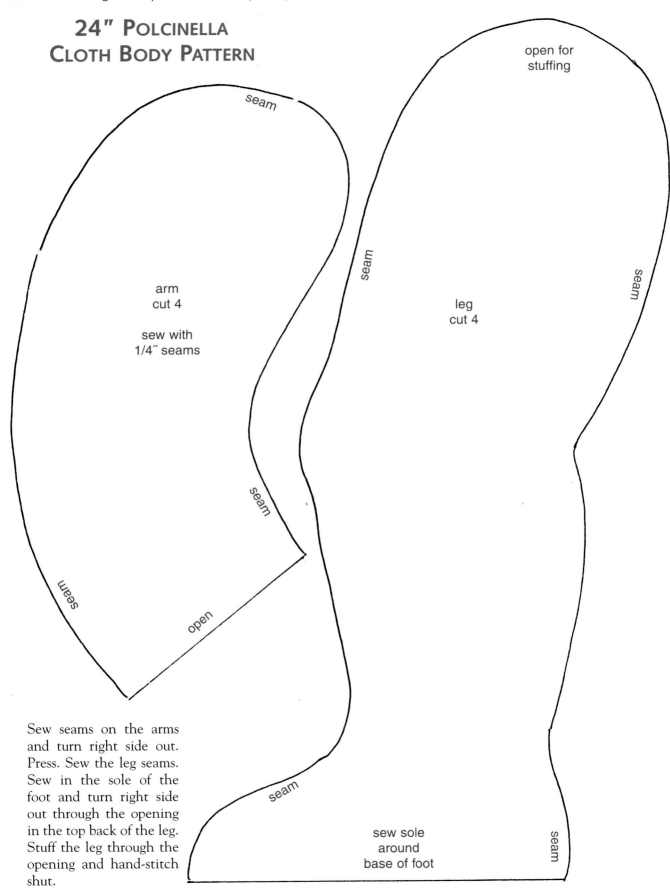

seam

arm
cut 4

sew with
1/4″ seams

seam

seam

open

open for
stuffing

seam

leg
cut 4

seam

seam

seam

sew sole
around
base of foot

Sew seams on the arms and turn right side out. Press. Sew the leg seams. Sew in the sole of the foot and turn right side out through the opening in the top back of the leg. Stuff the leg through the opening and hand-stitch shut.

Push the papier mâché neck down into the stuffed body and sew, securing with thread. The lip around the mâché neck keeps the neck from popping out. The head can be turned from side to side. After the arms are stuffed, put glue around the top of the papier mâché hands and push them into the cloth arm openings. Sew the arms to the body with a large needle threaded with extra strong button thread. Run through the arms and body from right to left and left to right and tied firmly. Sew the legs to the body with a large threaded needle run through the legs and body from right to left and left to right and tied firmly.

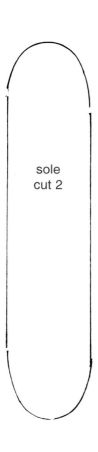

sole
cut 2

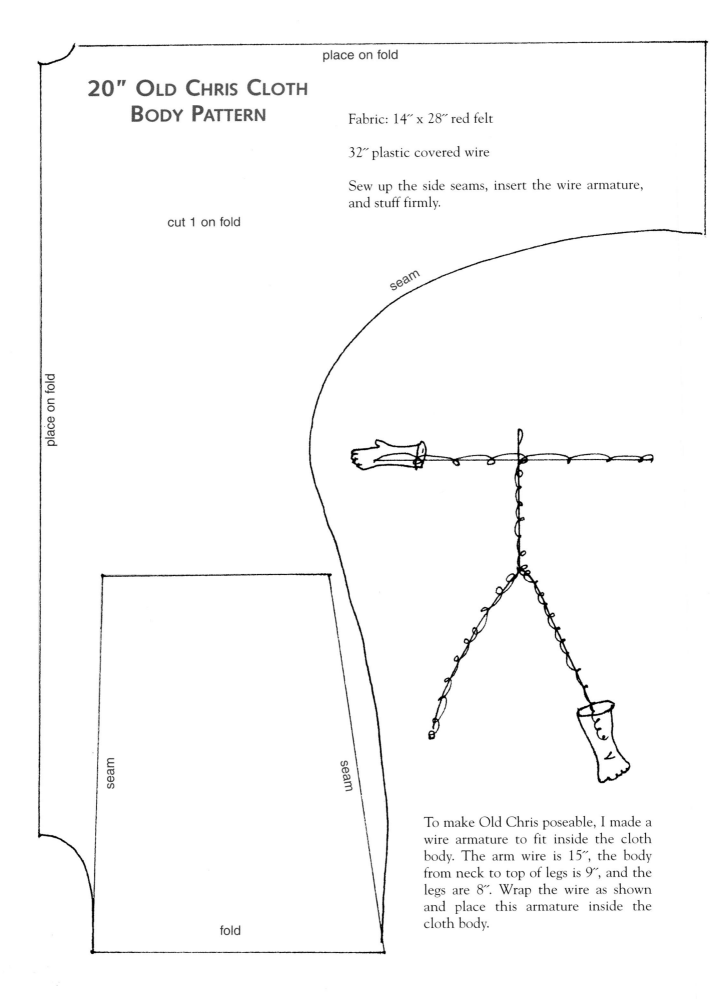

place on fold

20" OLD CHRIS CLOTH BODY PATTERN

Fabric: 14″ x 28″ red felt

32″ plastic covered wire

Sew up the side seams, insert the wire armature, and stuff firmly.

cut 1 on fold

place on fold

seam

seam

seam

fold

To make Old Chris poseable, I made a wire armature to fit inside the cloth body. The arm wire is 15″, the body from neck to top of legs is 9″, and the legs are 8″. Wrap the wire as shown and place this armature inside the cloth body.

Costume patterns

12" CHILD DRESS PATTERN

Fabric: 1/4 yard
Cut the pieces as indicated on the patterns.
Sew with 1/4˝ seams.

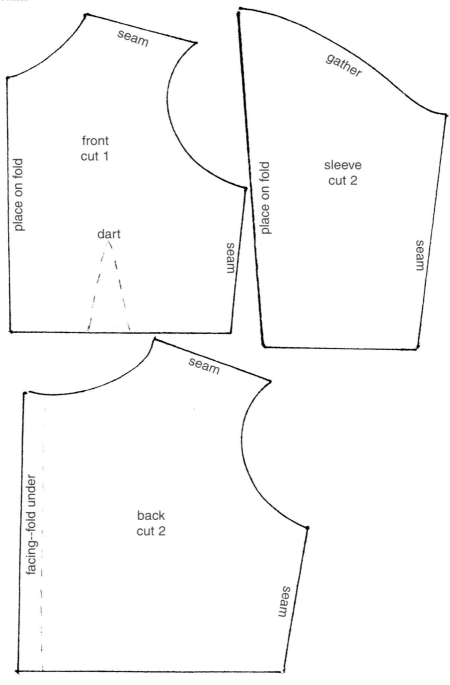

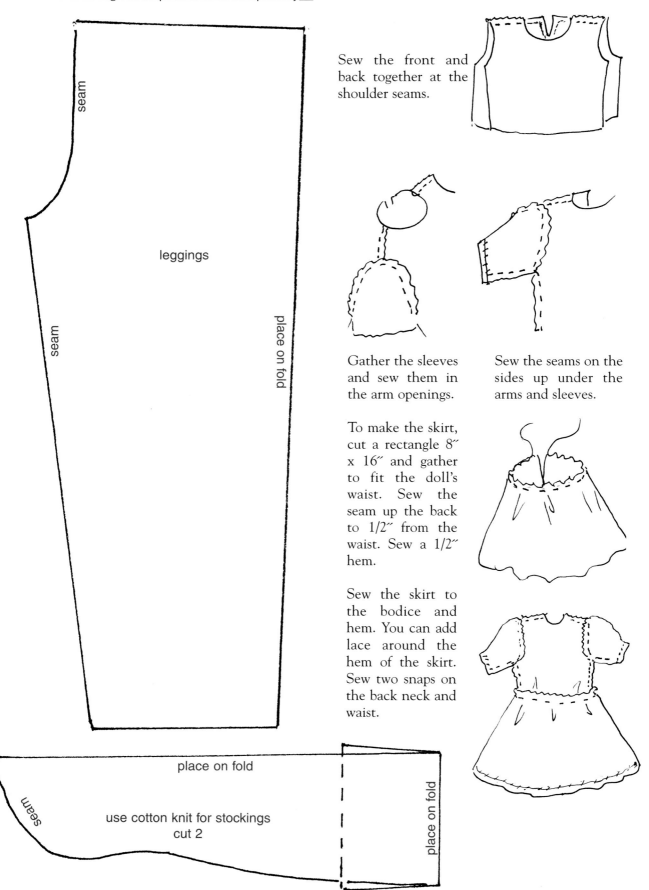

seam

leggings

seam

place on fold

place on fold

use cotton knit for stockings
cut 2

seam

place on fold

Sew the front and back together at the shoulder seams.

Gather the sleeves and sew them in the arm openings.

Sew the seams on the sides up under the arms and sleeves.

To make the skirt, cut a rectangle 8″ x 16″ and gather to fit the doll's waist. Sew the seam up the back to 1/2″ from the waist. Sew a 1/2″ hem.

Sew the skirt to the bodice and hem. You can add lace around the hem of the skirt. Sew two snaps on the back neck and waist.

15" CHILD DRESS PATTERN

Fabric: 1/2 yard

Sew with 1/4″ seams

Cut pieces from cotton, silk, chintz, or bastite in a small print or solid. Allow an extra 1/2″ on the front and back pieces for the facing. For the skirt, cut a rectangle 7″ x 20″ and gather to fit the doll's waist.

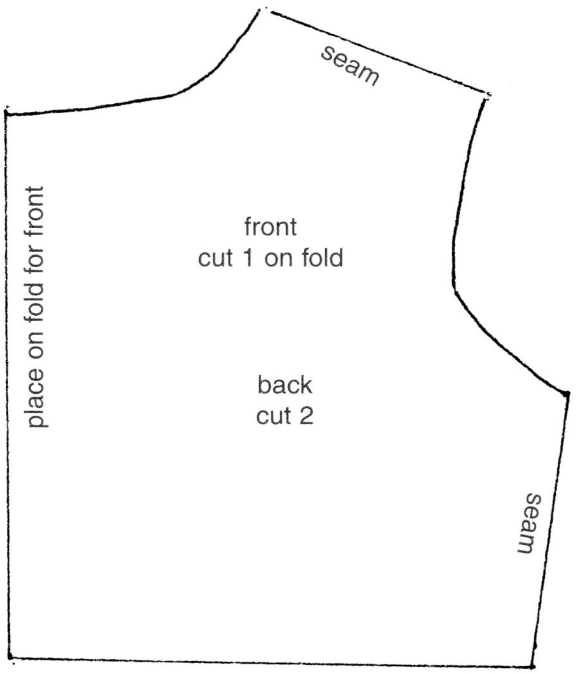

place on fold for front

seam

front
cut 1 on fold

back
cut 2

seam

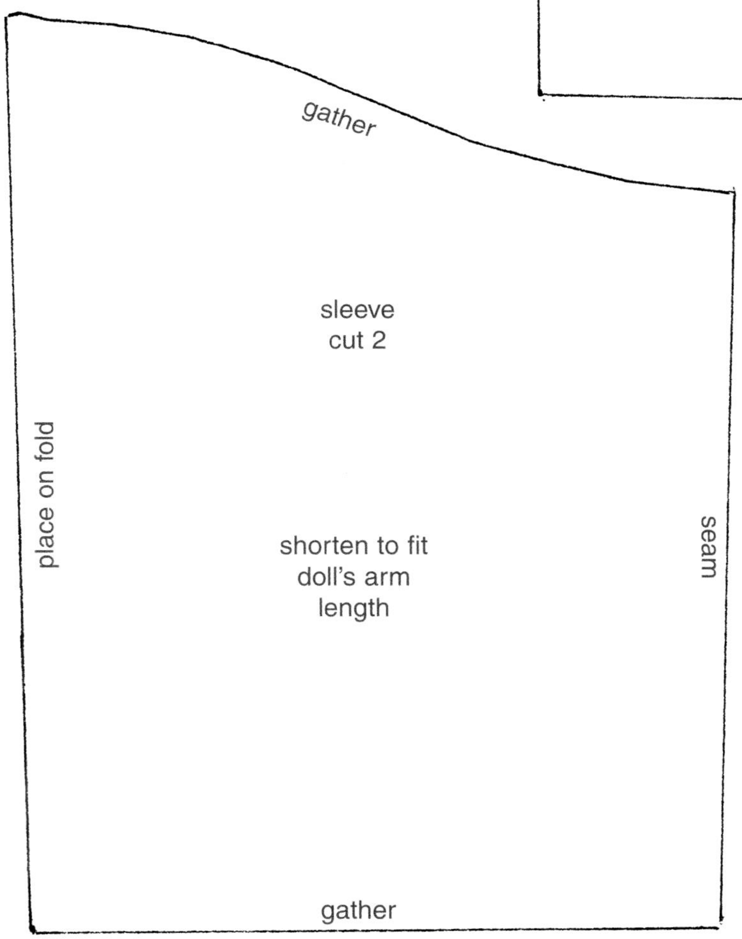

gather

sleeve
cut 2

place on fold

shorten to fit
doll's arm
length

seam

gather

15" Child Dress Pattern

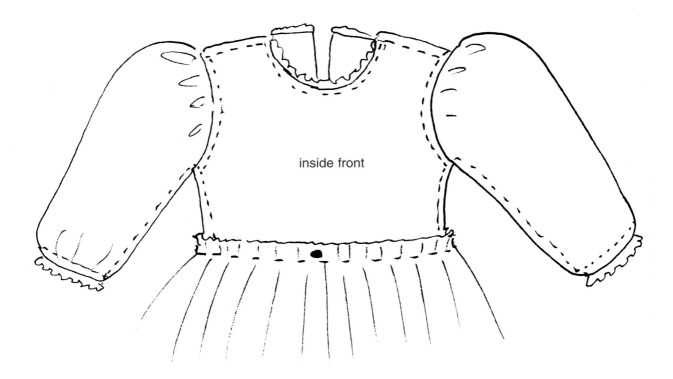

Sew the front and back together at the shoulder seams. Gather the sleeves and sew them in the arm openings. Sew the side seams and underarm seams. Sew the gathered skirt to the bodice and sew up the back skirt seam. Hem and add lace at the neck and sleeve bottoms. Hem the skirt and add snaps at the waist and neck.

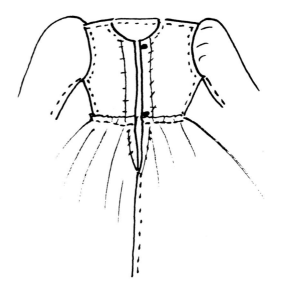

17" OLD FASHIONED DOLL DRESS PATTERN

Fabric: 1 yard
1 yard 1/2˝ lace
1 yard 1/4˝ ribbon

Cut out as indicated on the pattern pieces. The sleeve can be widened by an inch or more to both sides. Sew the darts as shown. For the skirt, cut a rectangle 12˝ x 45˝ and gather to fit the doll's waist. Sew the back seam and add lace at the hem.

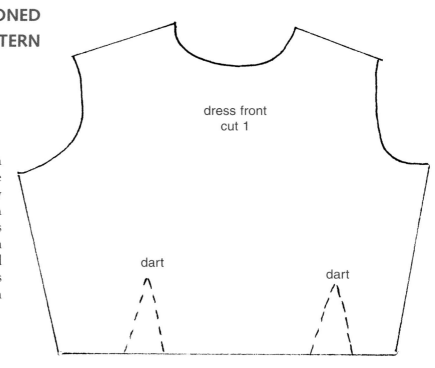

dress front
cut 1

dart

dart

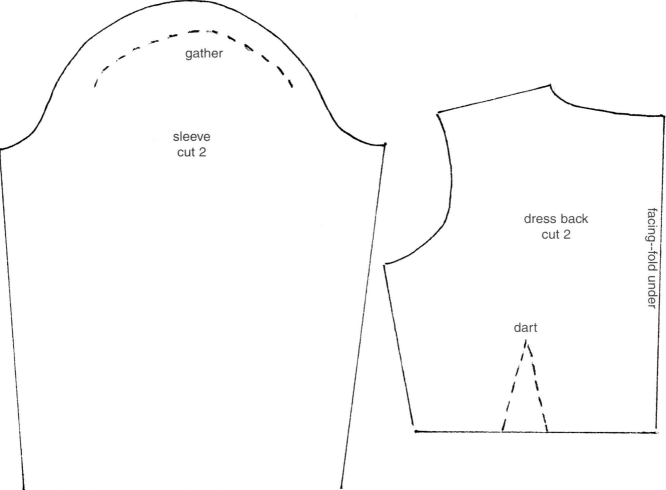

gather

sleeve
cut 2

dress back
cut 2

facing--fold under

dart

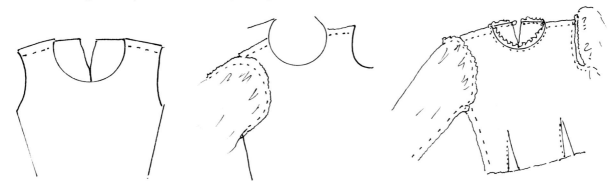

Sew the front and back together at the shoulder seams.

Sew in the sleeves.

Sew the side seams and underarm sleeve. Add lace at the sleeve bottoms and a snap at the waist and neck. Add ribbons and other decorations to go with each individual doll.

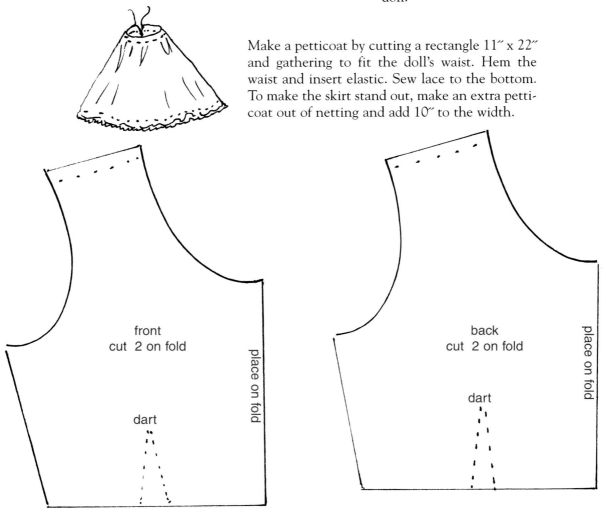

Make a petticoat by cutting a rectangle 11″ x 22″ and gathering to fit the doll's waist. Hem the waist and insert elastic. Sew lace to the bottom. To make the skirt stand out, make an extra petticoat out of netting and add 10″ to the width.

front
cut 2 on fold

place on fold

dart

back
cut 2 on fold

place on fold

dart

For a lower cut version of the bodice (see Beauty and Scarlett), use these pattern pieces. Sew in the darts. Sew the two front pieces together at the neckline. Sew the two back pieces together at the neckline. Join the front and back together at the shoulder seams. Gather the sleeve and sew in to the bodice arm opening. Sew up the underarm seam and the sleeve seam.

17" OLD FASHIONED DOLL DRESS

To make this skirt, cut the basic skirt for the underskirt and another 1/2 the length for the overskirt. Gather and sew both together at the waist and attach to the bodice. Turn right side out, hem, and add lace. Gather the top skirt in the center front, on each side, and in the back. Add a silk rose at each gather.

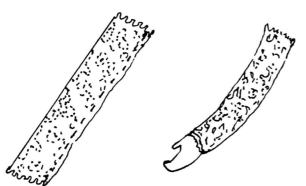

Make lace gloves using 5″ wide stretch lace. Cut to fit the doll's arm circumference. Sew up the seam and turn right side out. The seam should run inside the doll's arm.

Melanie's dress.

place on fold

CHINA DOLL DRESS PATTERN

Fabric: 1/4 yard solid silk or polyester
1/4 yard print fabric
gold braid trim

Sew with 1/4″ seams

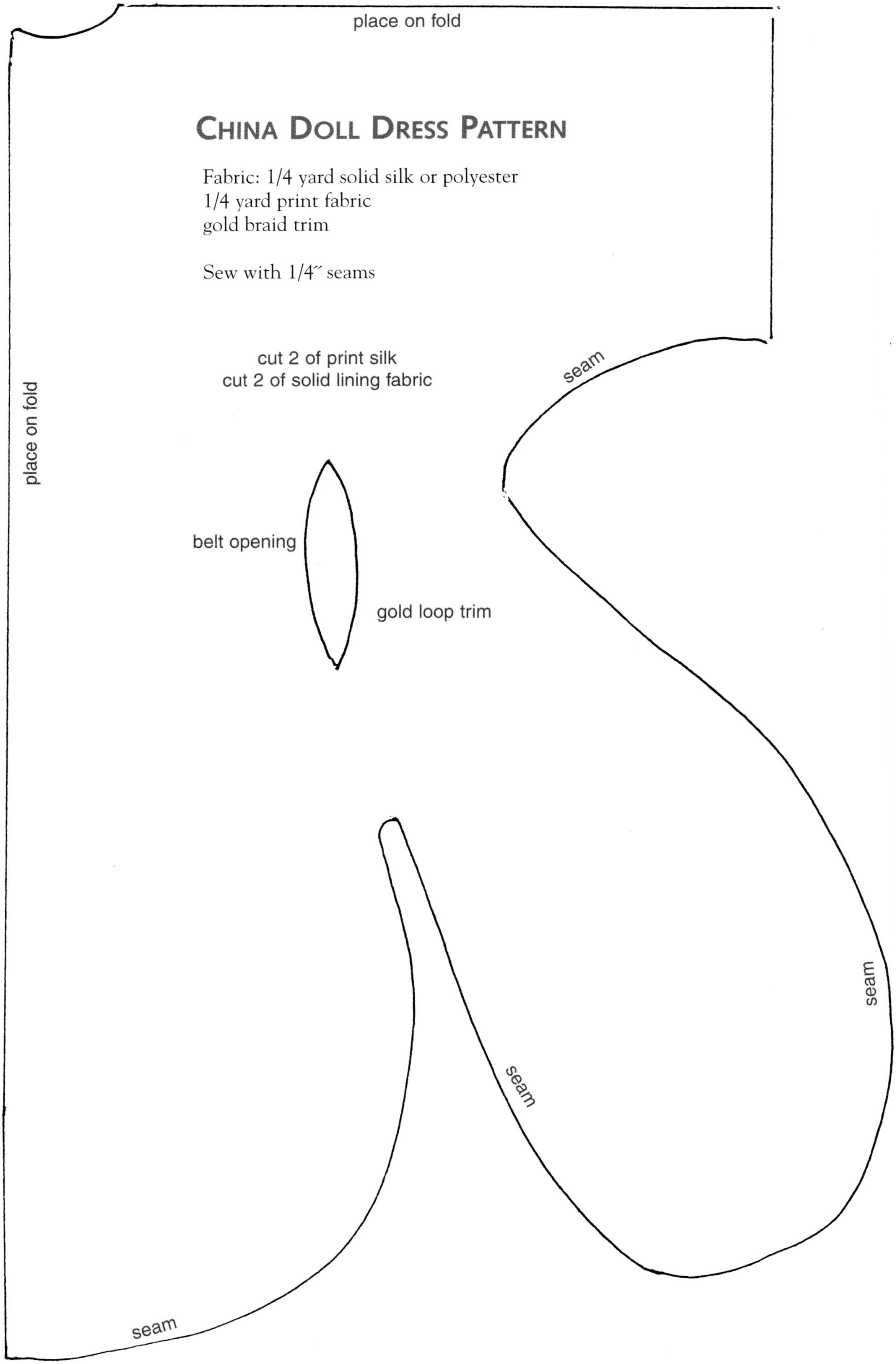

cut 2 of print silk
cut 2 of solid lining fabric

place on fold

belt opening

gold loop trim

seam

seam

seam

seam

place on fold

CHINA DOLL DRESS PATTERN

seam

place on fold

Fabric: 1/4 yard silk or taffeta

Cut a 2″ neck in the back only. Use hem tape for the hem, back opening, and sleeve opening. Sew gold trim around the hem and at the neck and sleeve. Add 2″ border of printed fabric around the bottom of the skirt. For the sash, cut a 20″ x 4″ rectangle and fold it in half, sew, turn right side out, and iron.

front and back
underdress
cut 2 on fold

collar of
dress

seam

fold

22" Doll Dress Pattern

Fabric: 1½ yard

Sew with 1/4″ seams

Cut out as indicated on the pattern pieces. Stitch front and back bodice pieces at the shoulder seams. To make the skirt, cut a rectangle 30″ x 36″ and gather to fit the doll's waist. Measure from the doll's waist to the hem and allow 1/2″ for the seam at the waist and for the hem.

For the Cala Vendor costume, you'll need: 1½ yard muslin or linen for the blouse and slip; 30″ x 14″ madras cotton for the bandana; 12″ x 36″ madras cotton for the shawl.

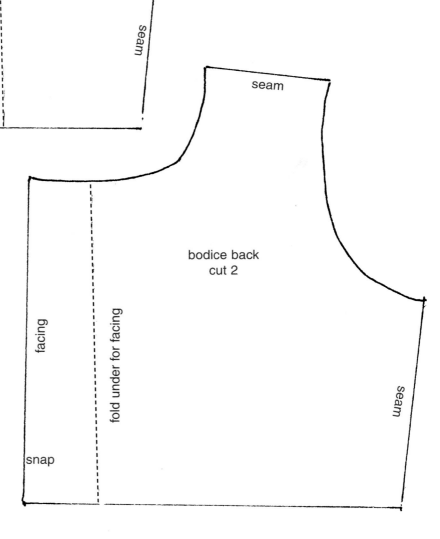

22" DOLL DRESS PATTERN

Gather the top of the sleeve and with right sides together, sew the sleeves into the armhole, matching the center top of the sleeve with the seam. Sew the side seam from the bottom up to the sleeve and underarm sleeve seam. Turn up 1/2″ hem on the sleeve, stitch, and press. For a fuller sleeve, extend the width 2″ or more on each side. You can make the sleeve slim or full, plain or with lace added. Fold the back facing under and stitch. Finish the neckline and add snaps at the neckline and waist. Sew the skirt to the bodice so the fullness is distributed evenly. Sew up the back seam of the skirt and hem. Add lace and trim as desired.

YOUNG PRINCE COSTUME PATTERN

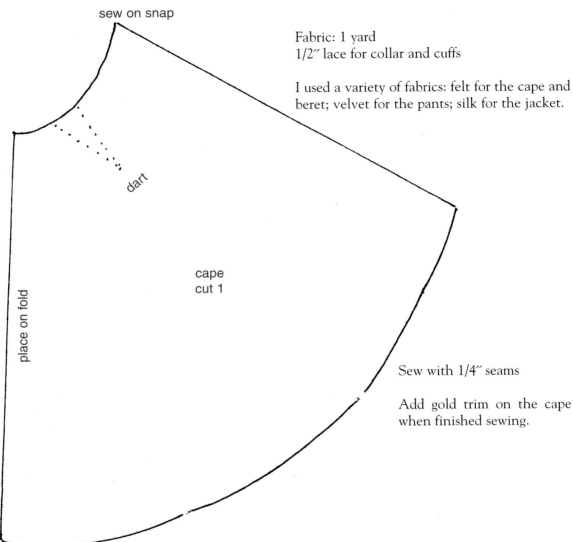

sew on snap

dart

place on fold

cape
cut 1

Fabric: 1 yard
1/2″ lace for collar and cuffs

I used a variety of fabrics: felt for the cape and beret; velvet for the pants; silk for the jacket.

Sew with 1/4″ seams

Add gold trim on the cape when finished sewing.

Cut out the circle, gather to fit doll's head, and stitch to 1/2″ piece of felt long enough to fit around the head for the hat brim. Add a feather.

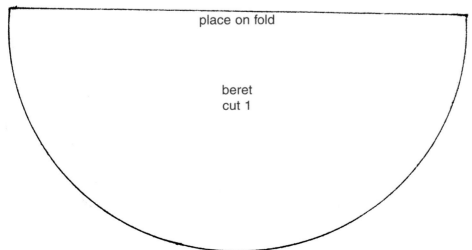

place on fold

beret
cut 1

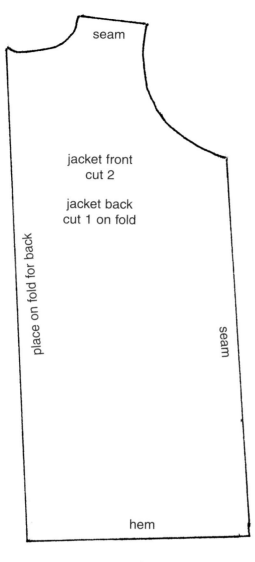

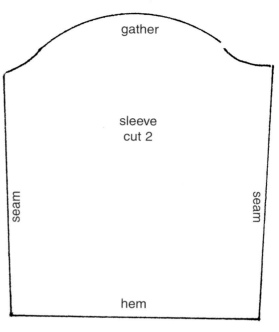

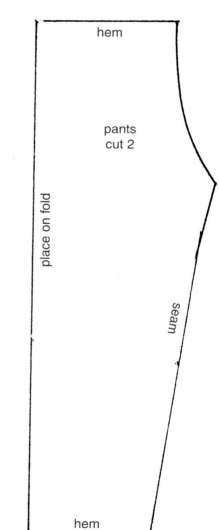

I made the Prince's shoes from velvet.

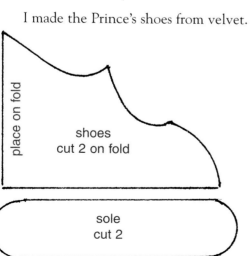

20" PRINCE COSTUME PATTERN

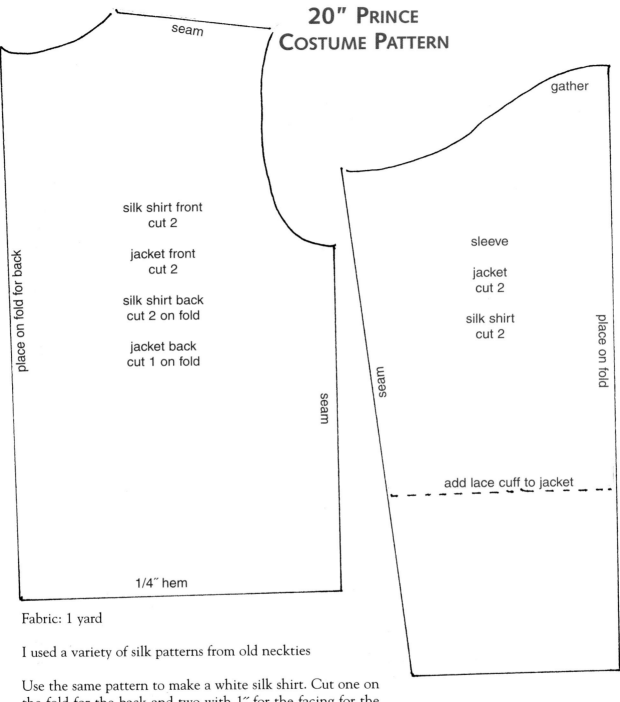

seam

silk shirt front
cut 2

jacket front
cut 2

silk shirt back
cut 2 on fold

jacket back
cut 1 on fold

place on fold for back

seam

1/4″ hem

gather

sleeve

jacket
cut 2

silk shirt
cut 2

place on fold

seam

add lace cuff to jacket

Fabric: 1 yard

I used a variety of silk patterns from old neckties

Use the same pattern to make a white silk shirt. Cut one on the fold for the back and two with 1″ for the facing for the front of the shirt.

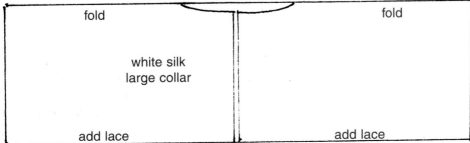

fold

fold

white silk
large collar

add lace

add lace

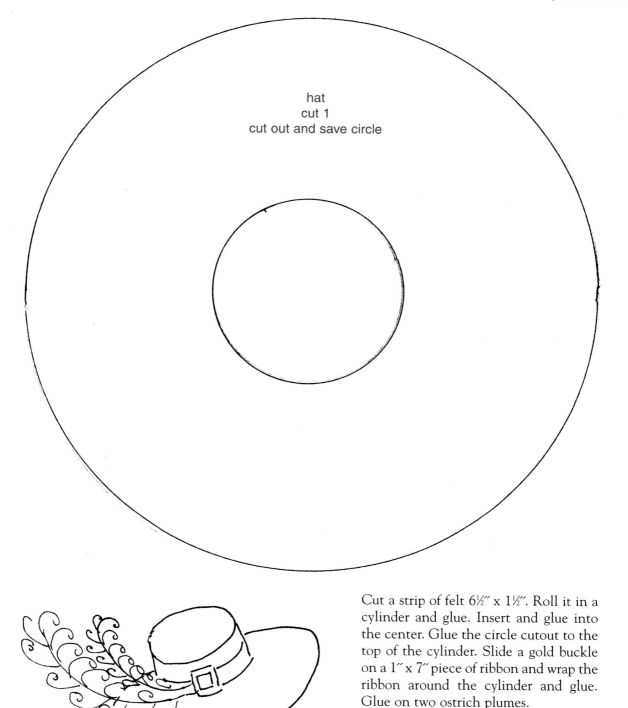

hat
cut 1
cut out and save circle

Cut a strip of felt 6½″ x 1½″. Roll it in a cylinder and glue. Insert and glue into the center. Glue the circle cutout to the top of the cylinder. Slide a gold buckle on a 1″ x 7″ piece of ribbon and wrap the ribbon around the cylinder and glue. Glue on two ostrich plumes.

The Prince is dressed in a silk costume made from necktie fabic, in the flamboyant style of the 1630s. A short hip-length coat, high-waisted breeches, long curled wig of brown mohair with a single lock of hair tied with a ribbon (lovelock) and a fringe of curls over his forehead. His beard covers a small area of his chin under the lower lip and his moustache is brushed up at the sides. A lace collar covers his shoulder and lace trims his shirt cuffs and stockings.

20" PRINCE
COSTUME PATTERN

Hem and add 1″ lace ruffle for the Prince's pants.

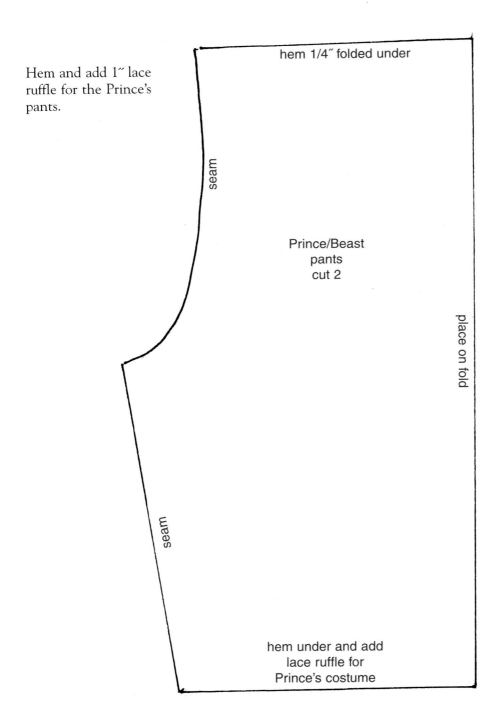

hem 1/4″ folded under

seam

Prince/Beast
pants
cut 2

place on fold

seam

hem under and add
lace ruffle for
Prince's costume

JINGLES COSTUME PATTERN

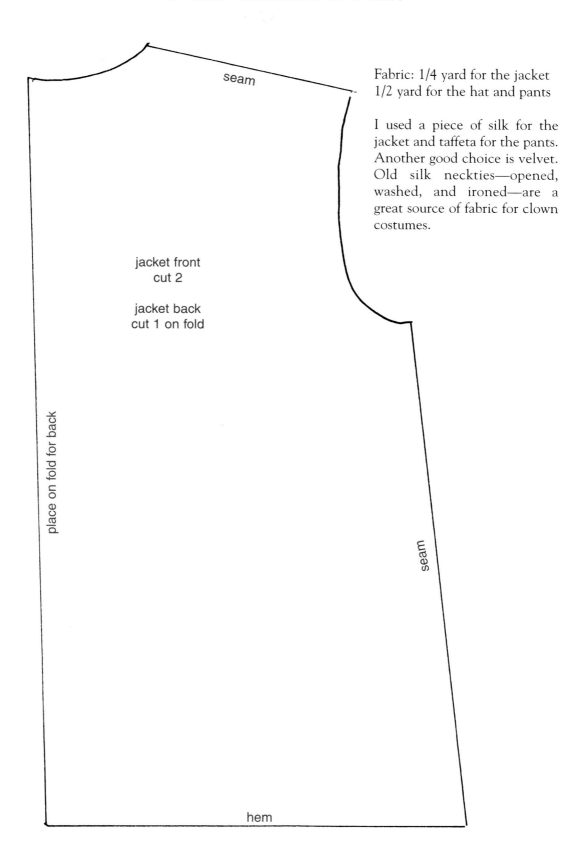

Fabric: 1/4 yard for the jacket
1/2 yard for the hat and pants

I used a piece of silk for the jacket and taffeta for the pants. Another good choice is velvet. Old silk neckties—opened, washed, and ironed—are a great source of fabric for clown costumes.

JINGLES COSTUME PATTERN

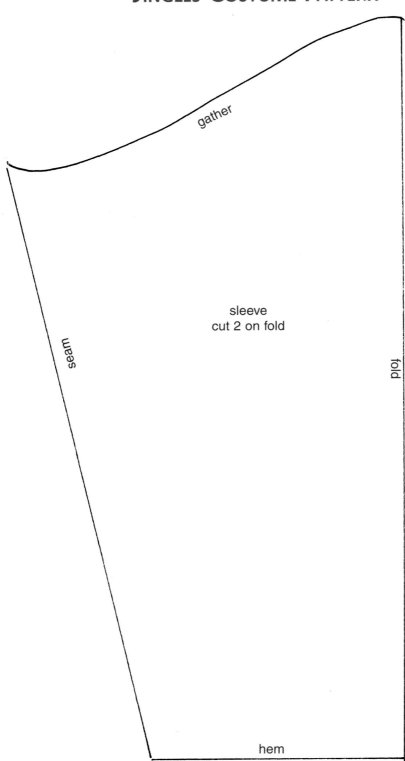

gather

seam

sleeve
cut 2 on fold

fold

hem

Jingles Costume Pattern

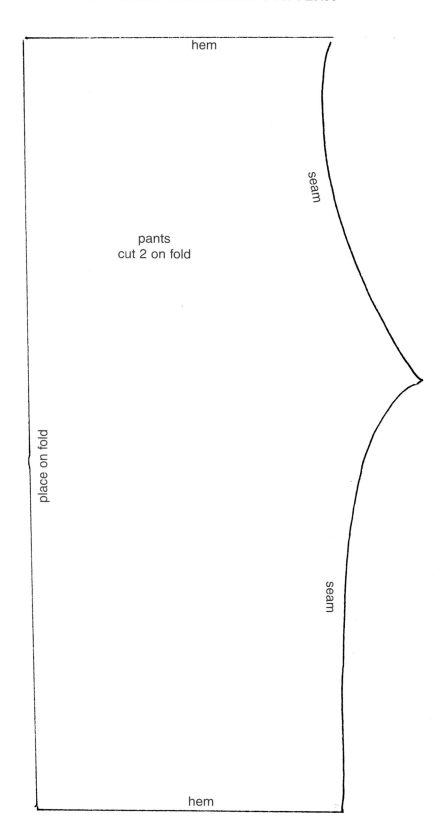

hem

seam

pants
cut 2 on fold

place on fold

seam

hem

JINGLES COSTUME PATTERN

Sew the taffeta front and back seams, then sew the facing front and back together. Join the facing and taffeta at the headband and sew, leaving an opening to turn right side out. Turn, press, and hand stitch the opening. Add trim, tassels, and bells.

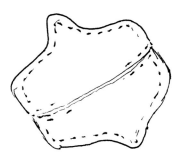

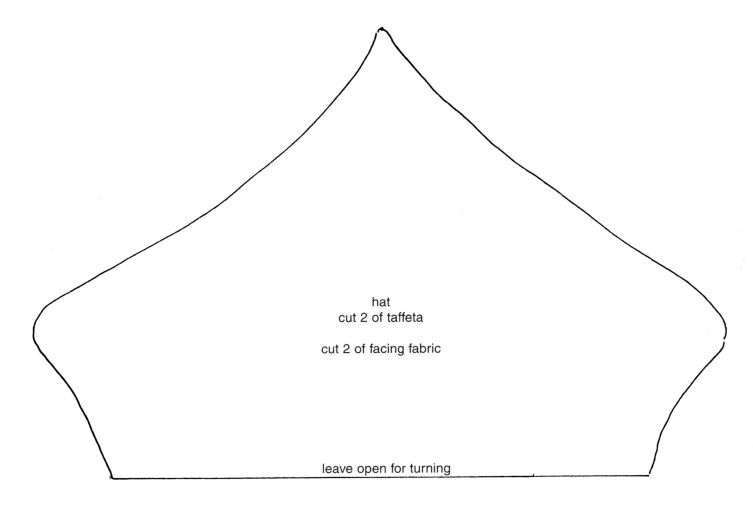

hat
cut 2 of taffeta

cut 2 of facing fabric

leave open for turning

OLD CHRIS COSTUME PATTERN

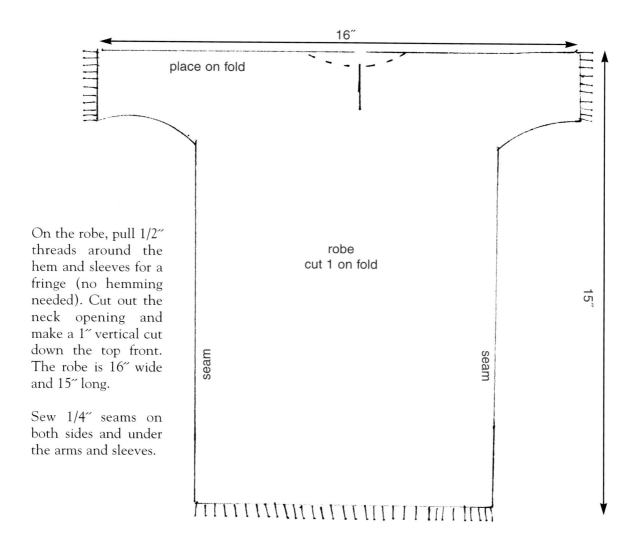

On the robe, pull 1/2″ threads around the hem and sleeves for a fringe (no hemming needed). Cut out the neck opening and make a 1″ vertical cut down the top front. The robe is 16″ wide and 15″ long.

Sew 1/4″ seams on both sides and under the arms and sleeves.

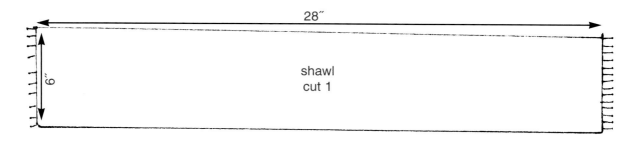

For the shawl, cut a rectangle 28″ x 6″ from loose weave wool and pull threads at each end for a fringe.

RABBIT VEST
PATTERN

Fabric: 18″ x 18″ white felt
12″ x 12″ red felt

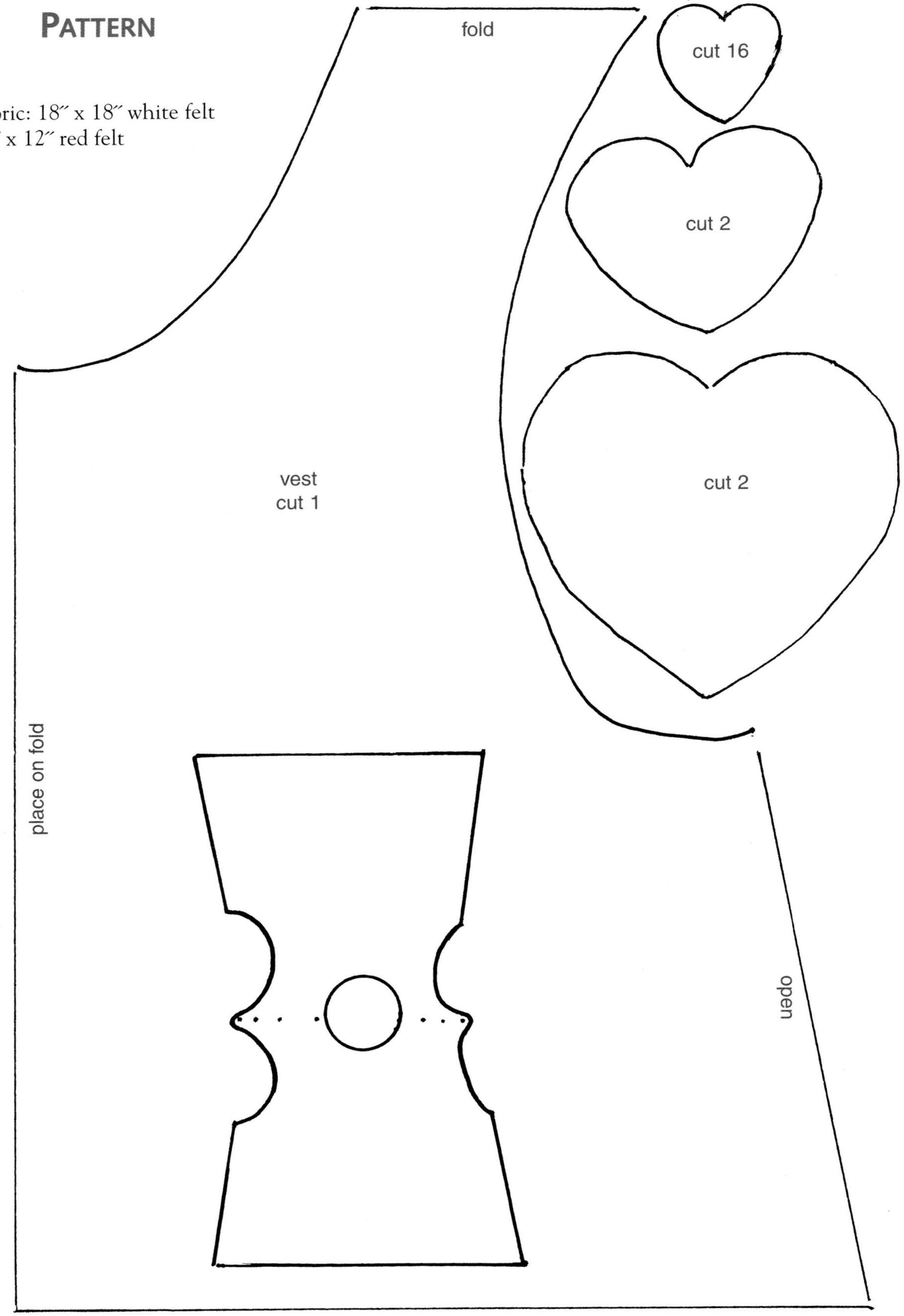

fold

cut 16

cut 2

cut 2

vest
cut 1

place on fold

open

The vest is open on the sides. Glue on the hearts and ribbon as shown.

Make a gold ruff with 4″ x 36″ gold netting and 36″ of 1/4″ wide gold ribbon. Gather the netting with ribbon to fit the Rabbit's neck. Tie the ruff around the neck.

Bring Your Creations To Life!